Mind Ripples

Published by
D'Har Services
P.O. Box 290
Yelm, Wa 98597
USA

info@dharservices.com
www.dharservices.com
dharservices@gmail.com
Ph:786 8374567

Art by Nina Tabares
Cover by Xiomara García

Contents

Introduction

The dream of every author is to see his or her work birthed in print for open, willing and hungry minds. "Mind Ripples" represents to the members of the Yelm Writers' Circle a gift of expression given to themselves, and to their family and friends. It is a legacy and testament of the rich and varied culture of Yelm extending out to the world at large. This inspiring volume of writings is for those who wish affirm their lives and for those who wish to enter at the fascinating world of writing.

In this anthology, you will find reflections that will keep the mind of the reader on a delicious edge: there is truth woven in fantasy and fiction, in the romantic and the irreverent. There are short and factual stories embedded with symbolism, prose interwoven with metaphor and simplicity. There is poetry that leaves the heart and mind of the reader soaring with new possibilities. All of this opens the doors of imagination, where the sky has no limits.

We proudly present to you: "Mind Ripples." With a sense of adventure, each one of the ten authors demonstrates a capacity to be versatile and imaginative. The more experienced authors alongside the novice offer you, the reader, a freshness of imagination and dynamism in each one of their writings and poems. Their works are delivered to you with the fecundity of the imagery language, while other authors present to you a narration that is enriched by local expressions brought from their countries of origin. From this, we grew, reaching beyond the limits of our preconceived paradigms of life and intellectual barriers.

Edilma Angel
Publisher & Pranic Psychotherapist
Author: Mujer de la Sombra a la Luz
www.dharservices.com
info@dharservices.com

Translated by:

Sanako I. Hurtado
Quantum Attunement
Author: Enchanting Nature of a Troubled Soul
&
Carolyn Chew
Healer and Author

*Go confidently in the direction of your dreams!
Live the life you have imagined. As you simplify your
life, the laws of the universe will be simpler.*

Henry David Thoreau

EDILMA ANGEL

$\mathcal{B}$orn in Colombia, is an author, Pranic Psychotherapist, and entrepreneur. Before moving to Yelm, she worked in the field of tourism with many years of experience in the area of Marketing, Sales, Planning and Management.

From 1981 to 1994, she was collaborating with The Inter-American Foundation «a foundation created by the Congress of the United States» in speeding up administrative matters and helping representatives and appointees of the foundations with itineraries and logistics.

During 1997, The Permanent Consultancy on Internal Displacement in the Americas, formed by organizations such as the United Nation System, Inter American System, Red Cross International Committee, International Organizations and Independent Experts of Technical Secretarial of Human Rights Inter American Institute «IIDH», did an in situ investigation on internal displacement. This activity took several months of intense and complex preparations, because it was carried out nationwide by two teams of experts appointed by member institutions. Being a self starter and a team worker, Edilma gave her professional, responsible, and capable support to the administrative and logistic organization of this project. In doing so, she helped with the success of an important and delicate issue.

While living in Miami, Florida, she pursued her love for art by studying Interior Design at the University of Miami specializing in Feng Shui.

Her great passion for reading since childhood has been profound and has resulted in an unlimited knowledge in many different fields. During the past 11 years she has pursued knowledge in many so-called non-traditional healing modalities such as Pranic Healing, Pranic Psychotherapy, Kriyashakti, Magnified Healing, Reiki, TRE and Blue Body Healing.

Edilma is Executive Director of D'har Services – Editorial Virtual of Literature wwww.dharservices.com and she has written a book in Spanish entitled *Mujer de la Sombra a la Luz* «Woman from the shadow to the light». It is a motivational book to help women.

Some of her poems have been included in the Spanish book entitled *Un Horizonte Literario* "A Literary Horizon". And Navegante de Palabras "Navigator of World". All books are available at www.amazon.com and www.dharservices.com.

info@dharservices.com

JUAN PACO

$\mathcal{B}$etween smiles and cuddles, Juan Paco danced to the rhythm of his mother's song:

"Juan Paco Pedro sing my song
Hear your name between my words,
I love the way I call you Son
Juan Paco Pedro sing my song,
Toola oola oola lo, toola oola oola lo"

"Down on the floor, and now up!" his momma said, "with rhythm baby, let's see...again...dance baby!"

"Ha Ha Ha" giggled Juan Paco

"Juan Paco Pedro sing my song
Toola oola oola lo, toola oola oola lo
Up! Down! Toola oola oola lo
Toola oola oola lo, toola oola oola lo!" Juan Paco shouted all along.

"Ha ha ha, ha ha ha" laughed the rest of his little friends in the neighboring cells.

"Toola oola oola lo!" one them shouted louder. Then another one softer, " toola oola oola lo".

And the other one "Tooooola ooooola oooooooola looooooo!"

The singing continued, until the new shift of guards came to their post, "Shut up fuck, shut up, stop yelling!"

The kids laughed while their mothers covered their mouths.

"Now ssshhh! Its bed time, they're going to punish me!" whispered the mother in Juan Paco's ear.

In the distance, they could hear the rumor of the sirens from the ambulances and police cars. They welcomed the nights amongst fighting, mourning and cries in the neighboring cells, while the women passed cigarettes to each other through the cell bars.

However, this day was different: Juan Paco was not allowed to participate in the morning check that would take him to the children's playground on the other side of the prison; his mother held on tightly to his little body, like she never wanted to let go of him. She cried tears over him, while her poor soul was breaking with pain. She knew that she would never see him again, for she was serving a life sentence. They will force her to part from him, and she had no other choice except to agree.

Right that moment, other hands where were pulling his body away from her, Consequently right this moment one woman was pulling her boy away from her, and she gave way, afraid that his little body would get hurt. With eyes filled with tears and a broken heart, she looked him in the eyes and told him,

"Forgive me son, God bless you and protect you my son, I love you. Forgive me, son!!!"

Dragged by a woman, Juan Paco cried all along. He did not want to part from his mother, and looking back at her he cried and shouted,

" Mom... Mommy... Come with me Mommy!" "Mommy! Where are you? I can't see you!" he was terrified. While the social worker tried to calm him down.

"It is alright boy, everything will be alright. You are now with me and I am going to take you somewhere else. You will be better there, and I will give you a present. Do not cry anymore, She told him.

"No, I want my Mommy! Mommy!!" cried the little boy. But, as they left the premises of the prison, the sight of the many unknown scenes in the streets caught his attention. He marveled at the different kinds of houses, as the car moved along the street. There were people running in every direction, cars of every color honking loudly, and then he saw the mountains, trees and long stretches of green prairies. Everything was new for Juan Paco, yet, his eyes reflected his sadness and his big brown eyes were swollen from crying so hard.

It was a long trip to get to the old house where he would find other kids like him, though he did not know any of them. He barely touched the food that he was served as they arrived; he was in shock and unwilling to speak. Juan Paco could not understand what had happened to him. Finally, he was taken to bed, for his journey was far from ended, and he will have an early start the next morning.

After a while, he fell fast asleep, but only to find himself startled in the middle of the night by the strange sensation of the lack of sounds in the environment. He could not hear anything; silence and stillness was something new to him. He thought to himself, _ "Where am I?" He could not hear the sounds of the women crying, or the wailing sirens coming from the streets. He tried to listen harder, but there was nothing to listen to. He finally panicked from the unknown experience of complete silence:

"Mommy!!! Mommy!!! Where are you?"

A nurse came to bring him a drink, "Take this little fellow, it will do you good. «Poor child» Stop crying, you are going to wake up the other children, and it still too early. Your mother is very far away now, and she cannot hear you. She will come soon, now be a good boy."

His face illuminated after her words and with a smile in his face, he asked "Really? She'll come soon?"

"If you are a good boy" she replied.

"Yes..." Juan Paco replied, while sniffing the snots from his nose. He took his drink and finally fell asleep, waiting for his mother to come for him.

The next morning the social worker came to his bedside, and approaching him very slowly, told him "It is time, wake up Paco"

"Mom! Mommy!" replied the boy anxiously, while vigorously rubbing his little eyes.

"I am not your Mother" said the woman, "But you will see her soon. Now, let me help you change your clothes"

They proceeded to get on a yellow car, and immediately left on their way to the airport. Paco was holding on to a lollipop and watching everything on their way with the utmost astonishment. He thought himself dreaming, while observing the many people driving different types of cars, wearing nice clothes and big smiles on their faces. The houses were colorful as well; their doors and windows, and some men working in the fields while children played and waved good-bye to the passing cars.

When they arrived to the airport, Juan Paco was curious about the different sizes of suitcases. He wondered to himself " What do they carry on those? And, what are they used for? I wonder if they keep little fairies in them?"

Shortly after, they arrived to an area where there were many rows of seats. Through the window, Paco admired in complete awe the gigantic plane stationed in front of him. With mouth and eyes wide open, he exclaimed,

"Look Mommy! Look at that plane!" and just right then, he came back to the harsh reality of his present situation.

"And where is my mommy?" he asked with eyes wide open.

"You will see her soon, be patient" And taking him by the hand, he was boarded into the plane he had seen through the window, while he quietly allowed them to take him to his unknown destination. Everything had changed. He was seated, and strapped on to the chair.

He looked out the window, and saw the men carrying the suit cases he thought were loaded with fairies. He then heard a very strong sound that he could not identify as the plane started to move:

" Mommy! Mommy!" he yelled in panic.

" It's alright Paco, you will see her soon"

His tears rolling down his cheeks. The plane took off and he held on fiercely to the lady's hand.

" Son, this is a plane and you will fly like a bird. There is no need to be afraid. You will like it" She told him, while Paco began to understand that this was a new adventure for him. Here he was, inside a huge plane that was flying up in the sky. Soon the sounds started to diminish and as he looked out the window, he saw many houses and buildings, down there, and there were so many of them...

"Look!" he said " They look so small, good bye! Good bye! Ha ha ha" He waved at the houses, yet, at the same time Juan Paco looked back at the lady, both afraid and surprised at the same time.

"Ah! Look! It's cotton, cotton! Ha ha ha!" Paco said to her

"No, Paco, it is not cotton. Those are called clouds." Replied the lady.

"No! It's cotton! Lots, lots of it!" argued Paco, unwilling to believe the woman.

Juan Paco rubbed his little eyes, and he opened and closed them very fast. He thought that he was dreaming, and spent most of the time looking out the window checking out the cotton balls. A flight attendant came and offered him cookies, crayons and paper to draw. He noticed her blue eyes:

"Are you and angel?" He asked, "My mother told me that angels have blue eyes. Are you taking me to see my mommy?"

The flight attendant knew that he was being given in adoption, so she gave him a tender smile and replied, _" Your mother will be waiting for you and we will soon be arriving at our destiny. Now be a good boy and make a nice drawing"

Juan Paco was confused with so many people around him and listening to new words that he did not know.

"I will draw something for my mother and I will give it to her as soon as I arrive. Yes, I will!"

He worked on his drawing for a while, until finally he was too tired to continue. He leaned against the window, and looking at the cotton balls, he fell fast asleep.

"Mommy, mommy!" He saw his mother smiling at him and wrapped in a halo of light.

"Yes my sweet dream" She replied to him

Juan Paco felt like he was being held by the tenderness and soft rocking motion of his mother's embrace. He felt happy while his mother kissed him and sang once more to his ear:

"Sleep my lovely child
the time has come tonight
to close your eyes and fly
tomorrow you may play
but now to dream you sway
hoola hoola lay, hoola hoola lay"

A smile painted in his lips, Juan Paco slept in bliss.

"Mommy, can you see the cotton? We are flying over cotton," he said to his mommy.

"My son, those are clouds in the sky; they move, come and go gently pushed by the winds. They will always carry you a message from me. Do not you ever forget that my son" The mother told him.

"Mommy, can I eat them?" he asked

"No baby, even though they are big and look like cotton, they are not sweet like the pink cotton that you eat."

There was a sudden and loud noise that brought Juan Paco back from the dream. He realized he was no longer between the cotton, he now could see the houses down below and something even more impressive and way too big; it was like a very dark blue sky.

"My mommy was singing to me. Where did she go?"

"Juan Paco, it was just a dream. She is not here, she is waiting for you" the woman replied.

"But, I want my mommy" Juan Paco said

"It is alright son. Here, eat this chocolate. You will like it a lot. Now, show me your drawing"

The boy showed his drawing to the lady, and there was a horse, a rainbow, a star, the sun and a little chicken.

Lost in his dreams, he remembered very vividly the games and songs that he learned from his mother.

"Mommy used to play with me" he continued, "she made me laugh and she taught me how to sing, like this:"

"The little horses go around the sky,
they fly, and fly, and fly, and fly"

«Juan Paco moved his arms with the rhythm of the song; his hands flapping like wings» He continued the song,

"The little chickens in the field
they peck, and pecked, and pecked"

«He continued to move his little hands and fingers, as if mimicking chicken pecks »

"The little fishes in the sea
they swim, and swim, and swim, and swim"

«He continued describing the movement of the water, and the movement of fish in the water, with his little hands»

Then, he turned to the woman next to him, and said: "Did you know that my Mommy named me after this song?"

"Juan Paco Pedro sings my song
Hear your name between my words,
I love the way I call you Son
Juan Paco Pedro sing my song,
Toola oola oola lo, toola oola oola lo"

Then, the boy became frightened when he heard another sudden and loud noise, though it was just the plane landing. All the passengers got up from their seats, and quickly rushed to disembark the plane. Even he got his security belt undone. The moment he was out of the plane, he felt very hot; this was something new to him, so he asked:

"Is this hell?"

"No, hahaha, who told you that? This part of the country is very hot this time of year. Come, hurry up they are waiting for you." responded the lady.

"Who? My mommy?" Juan Paco asked.

He did not receive an answer from the lady. Instead, she kept dragging him along, moving fast in between all of the moving passengers.

They got in line, and she presented the passports to the airport security agents. Everything was in order, so they kept walking until they reached a hall filled with bright light and many people. «He does not know. He will be living in the united States».

Juan Paco was speechless in the midst of his confused mind. He looked around, everything was new! Right then a very tall gentleman appeared in front of them. Juan Paco thought he looked like a giant bear! Though this bear had a big smile in his face. He felt intimidated, but then he noticed the lady next to him, and right then he was shocked by the sight: Her eyes were so blue, super blue! She looked like a complete angel. Her golden hair was down on her back, falling in a cascade of soft and gentle curls. She was really beautiful, and she was openly greeting Juan Paco with a big smile. She reached for his face, and with a gentle caress, she opened up her arms to embrace him, while slowly bringing him closer to herself and embrace him.

"Welcome home baby!" she said to him in "English", a language that he could not understand, for his only known language to that moment, was Spanish. Juan Paco thought to himself, "Yes, she is an angel. She doesn't speak like me" He opened and closed his eyes in admiration, not knowing what to do, when all of a sudden tears rushed to the corner of his eyes. The beautiful lady embraced him gently, and he almost felt, again, the sweet embrace of his mother. This angel... smelled really nice.

The bear man gave him an American football ball, "It is for you!" he said, but Juan Paco did not want it. Instead, he pulled the arm of the lady that had traveled with him, and said to her:

"Here is another person that does not know how to speak"

The lady took her time to translate Juan Paco's remark to the couple and they all laughed.

He looked at them puzzled, and thought they were all silly as well, «he remembered the word his mommy used to say»

"Juan Paco, these people are your new parents. Your mother sent you so that they could take care of you." Said the lady in clear Spanish, but Juan Paco yelled back at her:

"Mommy! No! I want my mommy!" There were tears rolling down his cheeks. He had forgotten about her in the midst of everything new around him.

"No, son" the lady continued, "you will remain here in the United Stated for a while. If you behave well, maybe one day you will see your mother again." She caressed his hair, turned around and left.

The boy felt the angel lady take him by the hand. He was hungry and thirsty his mouth was parched. The couple looked at him with eyes of love, and the bear man finally understanding put his fingers in his mouth and said:

"Are you hungry?"

The angel lady was looking at something in a book, and then, she finally said to him in his own language, Spanish:

"¿Comer?" «"To eat?"» she signaled, while putting her fingers in her mouth like her husband had just done.

"¿Si?" «"Yes?»" she asked again in the boys language.

Beber «"To drink? "¿Si?" « Yes?"» she asked while making a signal to her husband.

She finally ventured and said to Juan Paco, in Spanish, "Yo, mamá tuya" «"I am your mother"» she moved her arms signaling to him, "Yo, mama" «"Me, your mother"» she repeated.

Then finally, Juan Paco understood, "You spoke like me!" he said in amazement.

"Papá tuyo" «"He is your father"» the lady continued in Juan Paco's language.

"Mom and Dad" she said, while they pointed at each other.

"Those are strange names," thought Juan Paco, "Mom and Dad" he repeated with a soft and gentle voice.

He noticed the bear man walked away down a hallway and went into a nearby room. He thought to himself:

"Boy, angels have strange names. Why do they talk like that?" Not knowing what to do, Juan Paco looked around noticing how clean and brilliant everything was. The lights looked like stars. This had to be the "beautiful sky" of which his mommy spoke to him many times. He also felt the warm grip on his hand from the angel lady whose name was Mom.

All of a sudden, the bear man came back holding in his hand a big ice cream cone with cookies and strawberries drizzled with red syrup. Juan Paco's stomach growled and his mouth became watery. The bear man smiled and offered him the ice cream. Juan Paco opened up his mouth in total disbelief and said,

"Para ti" «"For you" »

Yet, Juan paco wondered to himself: " is that all for me? For me alone?"

They couple did not have to insist. He was fast eating the ice cream, while taking a mental note that he had never tasted something like this before. Never before! He was devouring the ice cream cone. He heard laughter, and words that he could not understand, but he was so absorbed in his ice cream that he did not notice the young woman that appeared and started a conversation with mom and dad while she looking at him with warmth in her eyes. She noticed how the boy worked on the ice cream non-stop while licking his lips over and over. In perfect Spanish the young lady said to him:

"Welcome to the United States. Your parents say that they will be very good to you. You will have a different life here and very soon, you will learn to speak English. You will go to school as well, though in the meanwhile, I will teach you. My name is Blanca and we'll be going home soon where there are many surprises waiting for you."

The boy looked at her with fear in his face, but the young lady reassured him.

"Don't be afraid. Everything is alright. These are good people, and they will love you very much. You will be able to eat many delicious things."

"I will be able to eat more?" he asked, while looking at everything with astonishment in his eyes.

"Yes!" Blanca said, "Many more things. Delicious things"

Juan Paco arrived at a new world. He lived with the angels who laughed at everything. They never got angry and never made him shut up. He had toys that he never dreamed of. A room just for himself and a pool...and then, one day...he found the sand! And it was really hot:

"Ahh!" he exclaimed. He looked happy as he played and played in the sand. When he approached the immensity of the ocean, he opened his eyes and said:

"Is all of that water?!"

He did not know that something that big could move like it did. The ocean played with him and threw him in the sand. Little Juan played very happy.

"It is salty! It is salty!" he exclaimed.

He remained quiet, remembering the warm soup that his mommy used to cook for him during the cold and rainy afternoons back in his country of origin. During those afternoons, he could not go out and play with the other kids.

"I will make a little house for mommy, yes! Ha ha ha! Yes!"

He worked the sand with his little hand, with a big smile in his face. The waves from the ocean coming and playing with the boy, bringing down the work his little hands where doing.

"No, don't do that. This is for my mommy," he said to the ocean.

Very soon, he had imaginary friends with him. His lips describing the same smile... while he would come up with new games. He laughed aloud with his mommy from yesterday ever present in his mind. He continues his life unable to fend for himself, at least not yet. He does not understand what happened to him; he is filled with unanswered questions, and the cries from his mother and the other inmates will forever remain in his memory.

The sounds of the sirens, the cold cells and the many nights that he heard his mommy cry. Memories...he would forever remember his mommy. She taught him the art of dreaming and the art of singing:

"Sawdust in the wind,
as the tree moves ding a ding
little creatures in the green
sing a song for dancing trees
ding a ding, ding a ding

sing a song for dancing trees.

Sawdust in the wind,
as the tree moves ding a ding
little creatures in the green
sing a song for dancing trees
ding a ding, ding a ding
sing a song for dancing trees.

Sawdust in the wind,
come and sing this song with me
sing a song for dancing trees
ding a ding, ding a ding
sing a song for dancing trees."

The boy sang the song while playing in the sand; his adoptive parents admired him greatly for this, and they felt a deep respect for the woman living behind bars back in her country. She had illuminated the life of her boy with the gift of music.

Juan Paco remembered how his mother gave him kiss on his tummy, while repeating "Sweet heart, sweet heart, sweet heart"

"My little baby boy
there's no sweet heart in the world
just as beautiful as you
my little baby boy"

"My little baby boy
there's no sweet heart in the world
just as beautiful as you
my little baby boy"

The boy was clever, he learned really fast. His parents noticed that from time to time he looked up in the sky, waiting for the messages that his mommy sent him. He knew very well how to decipher them, and his parents noticed this. They could see him smile and move his head in sign of appreciation for the messages.

Translated by:

Sanako I. Hurtado
Quantum Attunement
Author: Enchanting Nature of a Troubled Soul

ONE

When I am thinking in happiness
my mind sent to me
images of my beloved One.
You and your unforgotten smile.

The wind brings to me
voices and laughter.
I feel... I feel...
Gentle hugs around me
like a little one
into an innocent moment of tenderness.

The doorway
to the deep love and fondness.
Is this what we know as happiness?
Yes, it is.
You the only One.
You beloved Mother.

MONICA BROWNE

She was born in Bogota, Colombia. Her Parents were revolutionaries and atheist in a catholic country. As a teenager, she had contact with the natives from Amazonas; she participated in yage ceremonies, and spent many of her vacations in contact with nature and studying different philosophies. She always enjoyed writing her thoughts and sometimes poems. She studied Contemporary Danza for 5 years in Colombia, then move to Germany to continue with her studies. When she was in Germany she knew about Ramtha School of Enlightenment, then she move to Washington USA, to attend to this school. Currently she is living in a rural area, close to nature were she is enjoying gardening.

Blog: Naturaleza Universal
nuestranaturalezauniversal@gmail.com

WORDS FROM THE HEART

$\mathcal{I}$ am listening through my heart the words needed for this story... Pause... Breathe... Think, not think...

I think Everyone in the world has a story to tell, isn't that true? So if I were asked to tell my story, what would I say? Hm? Maybe what I am writingmakes no sense, but heck! Who said it needed it to!

So this will be my second attempt at expressing my own ideas with words and symbols that are still a little alien to me, even after 6 years of using them.

In my first attempt, I was writing about how people from different cultures perceive time in different ways... very interesting, but anyway that is another story...

This time I am endeavoring to write about my suffering... Ha ha, yes my suffering! Sounds funny, doesn't it? Well suffering, I realize, is like a big bag that I dare to say almost everybody carries within themselves, and yet are unaware of it.

I did not know I had it; but I do. And how did I see it?The uncovering process started one quiet afternoon, not long ago. On that day I received an email from a friend with a video in it, and in this video a woman was sharing her vision of life, and how she had healed her self... So, I pondered this for a moment and thought, "this may be worth checking into".

I found that she had also written a book, so I read her book[1] and answered all the questions, I also took the time to contemplate all the ideas that she was sharing, and it was in that precise moment that something clicked in my mind!

I encounter my suffering, I saw it, greeted it, looked at it... and finally, I accepted it.

And what I discovered was that that suffering didn't belong to me! It was merely my mother's belief system still imprinted within me. I understood that, this woman in her book said that when we are little we normally accept our parents' ideas or beliefs about life for they are our models of how life is supposed to be.

So when I was little, my mom loved to tell us her terrible and miserable stories of her life... alway at dinner time. «Or that is how I perceived it»

As a girl of only 6 years old, I was taking it all in. My mind was picturing every word she was describing. I saw the streets, the unkind mother, the drunken father, the nine siblings, the hunger, the sorrow, the thieves, the old house... all, just like when you go to the movie theater and you get immerse in the movie and you feel what the actors feel, you laugh when they laugh, cry when they cry, and so on... Well, that is how my dinner times were, full of the stories of her sad childhood.

Not only did I see all those stories so vividly in my mind, the

---

[1] *"You can Heal your life" by Louise L. Hay*

other important point is that the words were coming from my mom's mouth, so I was taking them as the absolute true. And when I did that, I literally pick up her bag of suffering and started my own journey through life, always using that bag's contents to run my life.

It was pretty handy, I have to say... it. Helped to me create many tears, ups and downs, lot of emotions, manipulation, victimization, poor me, and you name it.

Twenty-five years of suffering...

 I thought. "Ah, now I understand... why", lately it was getting very difficult to wake up every morning with excitement about life, to get out of bed loving life, and to be ready to start my day. Everything was cover by the dark cloud of suffering, because how could I see the wonderful things in life, if the only thing that I was allowing myself to see was the suffering of the world? And how terrible the world is out there, full of dangers waiting for me, ready to jump on me at any given moment. Now I know, it was all due to a borrowed belief system, nothing else.

So that quiet day was my day! I threw the bag away, and I am glad I did because it was getting pretty heavy. Then, I began to see my life with new eyes, remembering that life is beautiful, that life is all that it is, a miracle in itself, a work of art, a sweet melody coming from God.

"In the infinity of life where I am,
All is perfect, whole and complete,
I no longer choose to believe in old limitations and lack, I now
choose to begin to see myself
As the Universe sees me --- perfect, whole, and complete."
Louise L. Hay, *You Can Heal Your Life*

CAROLYN CHEW

*A*s a student of learning in the theater of life for the entirety of her years, Carolyn has found her interests to be directed to helping others and growing herself.

She enjoyed classrooms of wonderful children at the elementary school level in California before moving on to Intensive Care Nursing where she became skilled in working with patients in need.

For a different experience, she was in the business world of auditing hospital bills for insurance companies.

That work was great for traveling and meeting new people in several different states. She then moved on to integrational massage therapy, which included working with the emotional and mental aspects of her clients in California, New Mexico, Hawaii and Japan.

In the last six years since 2006 after moving to Washington State in the great Pacific Northwest, she attended an ancient mystery school. That helped to focus her love of soul and spirit, which moved her to a greater and deeper understanding of herself, and in the appreciation of the never-ending unfoldment of life's adventures.

Carolyn8chew@gmail.com

THE ANATOMY OF A FEVER

A fever burned through my body relentlessly and rendered me delirious. A couple of dear friends of mine had been alternately at my bedside offering sips of water to my parched tongue, and sponging my hot body with cool water for relief. This marathon of a fever came out of nowhere... knocking me down suddenly and completely. This, however, was to portend events that I could have never predicted.

It was at the end of the third night that I finally just surrendered to the 'burn.' I was beyond concern over what was happening to my body. I was drifting in and out of consciousness. Worn out, exhausted, I just wanted a cool peace in which to bask. I tried to relax myself, as uncomfortable as I was, but what really did it was rolling my eyes back into their sockets. I began to sense a floating sensation, along with a vibration that felt like fine champagne bubbles wending their way through my body. The sense of boundary around the 'me' and the rest of the world blurred even more, and then I heard a loud pop in my head, like a cork being ejected from its bottle.

It was really weird. I was suddenly aware that it was very, very quiet and really, really black...but it was alive, and scattered around were some very small dots of bright intense white light. I wondered what it was.

With that question, I saw against this unlimited blackness, the white light lines of an upside down U shape. There were maybe seven to ten of these U shapes in a row, with spaces in between them that made it look like a tunnel, with the U shapes as the infrastructure. Well, maybe they could be thought of as a series of arch shaped doorways. I didn't know what else to do, so I 'headed' for the first arch to see what would happen. Nothing. Nothing happened. At the second arch, again, nothing happened. Then, at the third arch, there was a 'whoosh.'

It was like it was waiting for me, because I felt like the archway was inhaling the 'me' that was without the body. As quickly as I was sucked in, I felt like I was being spit out, landing in a place where the air seemed like millions of tiny sparkling crystals. There were trees in greens I had never seen before, and earth, and shrubs, and beautiful birds. Most remarkable to me was the glittering air that was so alive and clean smelling. I took a deep breath, and my eyes opened even wider. It all felt so light, and the air caressed my skin with soft velvety whispers of touch. A grandmother Douglas fir tree seemed to beckon me, so I moved to her grandiose base that cradled me like a baby. It was so wonderful to feel this love, because there were still inside parts of me that felt unloved and unwanted. Those parts could receive from such a loving presence

I had been 'working' to be much less emotional in life because I was playing the revolving door of being angry, fearful, controlling, sad, 'peaceful', 'happy', and 'loving', so much so, that I just wanted stop it. I was dizzy with swinging. Enough is enough. How much more can I cry and blame someone else for my troubled soul? How do I forgive myself, and my family? How do I just be me, and being me is enough? How can I learn to love, allow, accept myself, others and life more and more deeply?

Comfortable in this Grandmother tree's arms, to my astonishment, I actually heard a clear voice in my head that said something surprising to me: "You have to remember that all you did, experienced, lived in all your emotions and thoughts is love, even if it didn't look like it, sound like it or feel like it. Even if you loved what was happening or hated what was happening. It is all an experience of love, this precious life of yours. We know we all have these experiences that are rotten or intense, and then we have these experiences that are just beautiful. And they are just ALL so beautiful, because we are alive and we are feeling it...the extreme pain, the intense pleasure and the infinite shades and nuances in between the two. We do not appreciate enough being alive. Some even call it a curse, and some even end their lives."

Upon hearing the voice say that what I was angry about was all love, and that my life was precious, I was startled...my unhappiness was love, and all the pain was love? Who, or what was this voice, I wanted to know.

The kind, peaceful and understanding voice heard my question and answered that IT, this voice, was an aspect of myself, and at the same time, a part of the whole, here to help me.

Then, to help me understand myself more, I was flooded with feelings and memories of what I considered to be a sad childhood. I was angry and withdrawn. From the age of twelve, periodically I would tell myself that I was going to end my own life, so then my father would be sorry for his meanness. I cried everyday for years because of that. To survive and deny my unhappiness and anger, I decided to withdraw from life in order to stay out of harm's way. I learned to be quiet, reticent, and took on the appearance of aloofness to hide my conflicted internal state. Such was the reasoning of a teen.

The voice then spoke: "For a time, you doubted all your experiences and turned everything into a big cord of pain, and you tried everything you could to avoid it. Instead of truly experiencing the moment, you, afraid of pain, attempted to fight it off. When you go around avoiding feeling pain, you end up not knowing how to engage life because you are not being present with each moment. The focus of your life, on a subconscious level, was to keep this growing ball of pain in check, for to feel it, was far too overwhelming. You were not present with each moment, because the pain of the past was mixed with the present moment. Thus, your life was colored and weighed with the unfelt moments of pain. Your consciousness became divided: parts in the present, and many parts in the past. So, the pain is a result of not being present with just the moment of now."

I wanted to really understand what the voice was saying. If I am present without the past, then each moment would be an experience, and there would not be any pain? Sometimes things are just painful though, it seems....

The voice elaborated more to me: "You know, it is like your friend said to you the other day, when she lived in her mind what the birds experienced when they fell dead en masse from the skies. She cried, but did not experience pain. I know this does not make a lot of sense to you, right now, but she, in her focus, became one with the birds, with no separation between her and the flock. She felt the intense energies of what was happening to them. She could experience the compression, the intensity, chaos, aberration and the horror of it, but it was not necessarily painful. Once the experience was over, there was not a residue of emotion. There was not the ball of pain of the past in your friend, coloring her being as she was one with the birds. She was present. Again, I reiterate, if we are not present it is because we have the memory of pain, and we keep building on this memory until it becomes something that we want to avoid all together. This can be done consciously or unconsciously. By doing that, ironically, we are just recreating pain, over and over."

In that moment, I was spun into a vivid memory of the past as if the voice was showing me what it was talking about. Some part of me screamed inside: "I don't like them. I hate them. Leave me alone. Don't. It's not right. It's not right that this happens to me or any little kids. Anybody, any kids." I could hear a part of me yelling, and I could feel the anger and sadness rising up inside, coming from someplace deep that I did not know was even there.

The voice, kindly and with a neutral presence, said: "Have as many long bad-ass cries as you need without judgment or shame of yourself. Say it all out loud without editing yourself. Feel it. Re-live it only as an expression of what was not felt all the way through at the time of the original experience. Be aware, this is different than feeding and perpetuating the emotions of anger, resentment, sadness, righteousness, etc. This is just to let it out, to complete the experience. Keep letting it out. The important part is, that you do not judge yourself while you are expressing. Remember in your heart that we are here to experience this earth plane."

The voice continued: "Experience. That word stands alone without qualification. So whether we judge the moments in our lives as 'good' or 'bad' really does not matter to The All

That Is, to who we REALLY are. It just wants to experience everything. It is your own guilt and doubt of yourself, and of your emotions, that blocks your way to having new chapters and adventures in your life. Self judgment is your worst enemy. We each are a part of the whole. We each are a cell of a greater body and our experiences add to the melting pot of the whole. It is as simple as that. So, to bring all the different parts of yourself into resolution, you need to cry or whatever, and just let the emotion be. I know you will say that sounds like self-pity. Really, whatever it is, it is just a motion of energy of your guilt, your shame, your doubt and lack, they are just motions of energy. To the universe, it is as it is because of movement, and that is the quality of joy that all of creation enjoys. No qualifications of what is, or what is not, good or bad. Just is."

Right in that moment, I thought to myself, "It is amazing to hear a voice in my head in the first place, but these words are most radical in my way of thinking. So, ALL of life, is a movement of energies and there is no qualification, no right or wrong, good or bad? What about violent crimes? What about murder and war? What about hunger and starvation of people, and most especially children? What about, what about..." my head was spinning with questions, and I could make a very long list.

Now I wondered if I was crazy for even hearing a voice, let alone what it is saying. After all, I had been feverish for days, and a bit delirious. But what the voice said next was even more mind bending: "Even though we are not aware, the All That Is, who we really are, enjoys the movement. Absolutely. The All That Is, is the quality of its non judgment, the is-ness of existence is the only quality it enjoys. Without the qualities of existence, it is the quality of itself without form, without any quality at all. It is of no-thing-ness. It is ALL there is...there is no beauty, no love, no joy, no grief, there is no sadness. There is no-thing, nothing. And so, in all of its manifestations, in its eyes, all is beautiful. No matter how it feels. No matter how it feels."

The voice paused, and I was glad because I needed time to take in what was said. All these years, I had focused away from my feelings, by stuffing them or altering them with my mind so I would feel better, and stop the hurt and the sadness. I never just let myself feel the feelings without judgment. So, we get to feel everything and it is all beautiful, because it is life. In the end, they are all just experiences. We are here living our lives on planet Earth and we perceive struggle. So then struggle is just an experience, love is just an experience, and ecstasy is just an experience.

What the voice says feels true enough, but I asked: "How do I resolve and get to the root of this anger so that I can be free of that?"

I surprisingly felt an expansion in my chest, and an energy like little champagne bubbles started flowing in my torso. In that moment, the voice kindly said, "Hurts, anger, resentments, sadness, jealousy, you have to let it all out, because if you suppress it, it runs you. It grabs and holds you. Be willing to feel without judgment."

"Even taking into account everything you have already said," I responded back to the voice, "Truthfully, I am afraid of pain. I am afraid of 'negative' emotions even though you said there is no bad or good. I am afraid of death. Because I am afraid, I play safe by not participating fully in life, and then judging whatever it is. I know that playing safe stops me. So, how do I move forward with these fears that are both unconscious, and conscious?"

The voice then went on and said something cryptic to me: "But, what I am telling you is that you are safe, if you allow yourself to do and to express exactly what you want to do in any moment. You do not need to hide from your fears. You are safe within your fears when you acknowledge them."

"How can I be safe if I am fearful? I do not understand," I countered, still in a quandary about how to resolve my fears.

Patiently, the voice elaborated: "Cry for yourself. Fear for Yourself. Just let the emotions be. You are safe when you acknowledge your fear and honor it, and you do not deny it or try to put on a façade of bravado. You then, can allow yourself to be who you want to be always. Okay? When you are authentic and real to yourself, you will respond appropriately to you, and to who you are with, in the moment. And who you are in the moment can eternally change... change is the movement of life. Sometimes just acknowledging the fear frees you up. That is an expression of you in the moment. If it is not expressed, it gets stuck inside as pain. I want you to repeat: I allow myself to be who I want to be and what I want to be in any given moment. No shame, no guilt, no judgment, just an experience and expression of myself."

"Yes," I said, "but I think I have to sit with these ideas a while. I know in my mind that fear is all illusion, but it is such a compelling one."

However, the voice reminded me once again, "So what if you feel fearful? It is only an experience. A moment. So if it hurts, it is only a moment if you are present with it. It is not who you really are. You are a soul and spirit in a human body through which you interface. Remember, to the All That Is, who you really are, all is beautiful because it is simply an experience, and no matter what it looks like, feels like, tastes like, sounds like, they are just experiences. Ultimately, there is nothing you can really do wrong or right for that matter. You can only experience."

I rolled my eyes on the ceiling, and said, "Aye, yai, yai! If all is really JUST an experience, then that negates the fear of being wrong, of being bad, of not loving enough, of a lot of judgments I have of myself and others. It appears as if life would be a lot more satisfying, happy and harmonious without my judging good or bad consciously or unconsciously everything... big or little. In each moment of my life, I get to experience and express... However, even though all is just experience, there are still certain things I would rather experience, and certain things I would rather not. So how do I reconcile these new thoughts with how I feel?"

The melodious, soft spoken and patient voice continued: "Feeling is important because we are here to experience what it is to be alive, even if it is painful sometimes. Just don't get caught hanging on to the way the experience feels. Allow yourself to feel so that you understand what it feels like to do that. Then, you will know more about yourself and your choice of expression. Allow all of it and practice to not defend or tighten against it. But this is not what you have been doing. You tend to modulate everything because you feel like you can get out of control, that you might hurt yourself or somebody else. That is judged emotional pain, not felt all the way through. That is the part that is afraid that it is going to hurt somebody. Just feel the feeling, and that means being able to watch it at the same time."

Still lying in the comfort of this grandmother tree, I realized that judgment of myself and others occurred because I felt so separated and believed that I was bad and unloved. I saw myself as entirely guilty for the experiences that I had. I sometimes thought of myself as wrong, a fraud, angry, sad, and contracted from fear. "Whoever or whatever this voice is," I thought to myself, "it is helping me to understand that all of life is life, and we can each make of it as we will...all is allowed. Still, even though my past expression was contracted, living a heartfelt life is what I would like to experience next."

The voice heard my thoughts, and with a most loving, sweet, and gentle tone, said: "Step into the beingness of heart. So, it is not about words. The words can go into the brain, the mind, but it is about your own experience in your heart. There is much you can resolve from truly opening your heart. Yes, it is the heart, to have the heart to experience fully whatever it is. Of course, at the very core of this, is to have the heart for yourself, because you are everything and everyone; we are all everyone and everything. Everybody 'outside' of you, is yourself. What would it be to simply love the one in front of you? How big can your heart be? Ask yourself. How expansive can it be to include all?"

With that, I felt a shift in the energies all around me, where I wasn't able to discern a me, or the Grandmother tree, or the sky. It felt like we were all each other as one; a gentle movement of life as an is-ness of being, woven in love. I basked in this new found peace, a peace that I had never known before. I can say with words that I felt love, I felt no separation, I felt no judgment, there was no thought, yet, words fall short. This, for me, was an experience that I would forever visit, again and again.

I thank the gift of this fever.

It's been nine months since the fever and I continually practice, over and over, allowing myself to feel more and more deeply. At first, it was daunting to simply feel afraid of feeling. Then, it was a bit disconcerting to not feel as much as I would have liked, because in the arena of feelings, I know there are infinite universes. With continued application, the treasures of my being are continually revealed, the more I allow myself to be present with myself, both publicly and in the quietness of my remote cabin in the woods. The voice was right in saying that once I accepted and acknowledged my fears, and just allowed myself to be who I was in the moment, I would find that the fears had changed, and the world did not come crashing down on my head. I am feeling more secure in myself, and I am changing to view the world with new eyes.

These days, I am more peaceful inside. What a wonderful way to enjoy life. The world events are still going on in the world news. Life inevitably goes on, and yet everything for me is more harmonious and less conflicted. I am more accepting, learning to love myself just as I am, loving life just as it is. Life is more fun...life is lighter...my heart is lighter and happier. Life is worth living just to realize that change can happen, and that I can be happy just being me, having experiences just for the sake of it.

ROBERT WILLIAM CORL

*R*obert is a Renaissance man. His life has been an exploration of experiences... biker, soldier, poet, actor, mathematician, and musician... a trained opera singer on the one hand... a guitarist and songwriter on the other. But above all, he has been both a student and a teacher, and the line between the two is often blurred. A lover of life and the world around him, his writing always seeks to tell the story simply, so that the reader may become part of the dance.

Tenor165@yahoo.com

THE FLOWER GIRL

*H*eat, humidity, and the aroma of a thousand cooking fires assaulted my senses as I stepped from the plane. Bangkok. I was really on the ground in Bangkok, although it was just a stop along the way to my undercover military intelligence assignment in Vientiane, Laos. It was January 1970, and the Vietnam War had finally interrupted my life.

During three years of college I'd had time to think about the war and how I wanted to handle it. Many close friends had already gone into the service. We were the sons of blue-collar workers, and we'd grown up watching John Wayne pull the pin from many a hand grenade with his teeth. We had seen every manner of war movie, from WWII films to Italian gladiator movies on lazy Saturday afternoon television. There was no question about whether or not we'd go—no war protesters or draft dodgers here. Our dads were vets, and we never considered avoiding the draft. We were too uninformed to protest, and too undaunted to run away when our time came. None of us cared much for Canada anyway.

The first meaningful Vietnam casualty I can recall was a guy from my high school. He was a couple of years ahead of me, and the small article on a back page of the hometown paper said he'd been killed in some place that began with a V. His uniformed photo appeared above the notice, which contained fewer words than a classified ad. Reports began to show up on TV, and as the statistics mounted many of us avoided watching the evening news altogether. I remember as a child growing up in the fifties, my dad, who'd been in the Navy, would watch *Victory at Sea* on Sunday evenings. Sometimes the documentary style became too graphic for me, and I'd quietly leave the room. Unlike the movies, those documentaries sometimes contained slices of reality my young eyes were not ready to see. Watching the evening news, with the death toll in Vietnam given as if it were the highway death toll statistics over the July Fourth weekend had the same effect on me. Hearing the number of Americans killed that day or that week in Vietnam began to wear thin.

On June 27, 1969, *Life* magazine published the pictures of a single week's Vietnam American war dead. The cover was a mass of little photographs, and each was described in a story inside. It was shocking to see page after page of bright young heroic faces, each showing such hope and promise, and to realize they were all dead and gone. I think the effect of that issue was to wake people up from the numbing drone of casualty figures. Putting faces and names to the statistics changed things. Sometimes I wonder if it would have swayed my decision to enlist, had that magazine been published sooner. I know the impact it had on public opinion.

By the time my turn came, all my buddies had warned me that it was better to volunteer for three years than be drafted for two. On the surface, that seems illogical, but the rationale was all too clear. Two-year draftees weren't going to be in long enough for advanced training, so they invariably went to infantry school after basic training and then straight to the bush. A three year volunteer could be given more training before going to war. With some form of 'specialized' training, a soldier had a better chance of coming home alive.

Some years later I shared this logic with a woman who had lost her first husband in Vietnam. I was singing for her second wedding. Her first husband was a two-year draftee, she explained. He had told her he just wanted to do his two and get out. He didn't make it. She was still bitter.

Based on what friends had told me, the choice was clear, so I volunteered toward the end of the summer of 1968. August and September were so hot and humid in Fort Bragg, North Carolina, that the Army had invoked its 'heat category 4' alert on more than one occasion, meaning there were days when even the Army knew it was too hot to train. We were grateful for any chance to get out of the scorching summer sun, even if it meant going into a darkened theatre to watch a film on venereal disease. When these 'breaks' were over, we'd return to our heavy M-14s and battle gear, all neatly arranged outside, and to our sun-baked canteens, now filled with hot water. So, at the end of basic training, my entire company was temporarily thankful to be seated in bleachers in the shade of some tall pine trees. We were about to be read our orders.

When I enlisted I had volunteered carte blanche. I could have picked a training specialty before signing, but I had no idea what to choose, so I left it up to chance, and as chance would have it, the Army was about to issue a nationwide call for intelligence candidates and I was swept up in that call. Now, as our duty assignments were read aloud, some heard the worst posting of all, "Fort Polk, Louisiana, Infantry School." Fort Polk was the kiss of death. It was the only place in the U.S. considered as bad as Vietnam itself, and it was a one way ticket to the bush. Others went to similarly awful AIT «Advanced Infantry Training» destinations, but when they reached my name they read aloud, "Fort Holabird, Baltimore, Intelligence School." No one in the bleachers heard anything other than 'Baltimore', at which point the entire company looked at me and questioned that destination aloud, as if on cue. No one was more surprised than I.

The Army has a phrase, 'hurry up, and wait', for a very good reason. It is SOP – standard operating procedure. It describes most duty assignments, and mine was no exception. First there had been a shortage of Intelligence candidates, and now there was a glut. Many were siphoned off to 'holding' companies in places like Ft. Hood, Texas. I was stuck at dinky little Fort Holabird for months – no job – no training. Finally, orders came transferring me to an Intel outfit at Fort Meade, halfway down the parkway to Washington, D.C. At the 528th MI we were trained by returning Vietnam veterans in the arts of interrogation, map reading and analyzing intelligence data and documents. Interrogation training was as much a survival course as it was the study of such things as the "Mutt and Jeff" technique «good cop/bad cop». These veterans filled our heads with stories. Some interrogators had become so violent that they'd thrown prisoners out of helicopters one at a time, until someone decided to talk. We were told how one of our interrogators had been killed by a prisoner who stabbed him in the throat with his own pencil. It was with a heightened sense of awareness that we knew our turn was coming, yet still we went nowhere – hurry up and wait. By June I'd been in the Army for ten months, during which time I'd had 4 months of 'hurry up' (training), and six months of 'wait'. While attached to the 528th Military Intelligence Company in Fort Meade, we got word that we, too, were to be re-assigned. Rumor had it that we'd sit out the war in Fort Hood, Texas.

Now, I'd never been to Texas, and the thought of getting to see the Lone Star State would not normally have been an unwelcome prospect. But I knew that if we were assigned to a holding company, we weren't likely to do much other than busy work. Given a choice to paint rocks «a typical make work project» and stand inspections in Texas, or go to war, what would you do? Right. Rather than get stuck polishing boots, saluting and painting those damned little rocks that border each barracks, I volunteered for Vietnam. I also volunteered for language school, and a half dozen other assignments posted on the barracks bulletin board. I signed up for language training in French, Italian, Chinese, Vietnamese, Slavic and more. My luck held, as my next assignment was language school. In the end, I got French because it was the prevailing European language of Vietnam and Laos.

Looking back on it, it's funny how one decision can precipitate a chain of events. For example, while in college I had changed my major to music. It was no big deal – or so I'd thought. In trying to audition for the college chorus, the staff music teacher, Margaret Franzone, had convinced me that I had a talent for singing opera. I'd been singing along with my Mother's Mario Lanza records, but I was ignorant of any academic approach to singing. Margaret suggested a change in my academic focus from secondary education to music education. It was a logical choice, it felt right, and so music became my passion. I even received a music scholarship when I transferred to Temple University in Philadelphia. However, this decision did not go unnoticed.

My draft board decided that anyone who had changed their college major was trying to prolong their stay in college in order to avoid the draft. Although I viewed my decision as a lateral move «after all I was still in the 'education' field», the draft board did not. The Draft Board changed my status to 1-A and tried to take me in the spring. They had to let me finish the semester, so I finished up and then volunteered after enjoying a summer of girls and motorcycle rides to the Jersey shore. When I walked into the recruiter's office on a Friday and told him I wanted to go in on Monday, he thought I was stoned. It was Friday, the thirteenth.

My parents took me to the old Reading Railroad station in Pendel, PA on Monday. As I waved goodbye, I had mixed feelings. My Mom was emotional because I was the first of six children to truly leave the nest. My Dad was stoic and made a few wise cracks, as usual. Now I can relate to how they must have felt, but at the time I could not have understood. I missed them already and felt apprehensive about my decision. Yet, I felt a profound sense of excitement at having thrown caution to the wind. Like a lot of young men my age, like those bright faces I was later to see in Life Magazine, I was full of hope and promise and this was to be my first adventure as a man.

At the induction center at 401 North Broad Street in Philadelphia, they inspected us to make sure we had two of everything we were supposed to have two of, and then they gave us a battery of tests. There was a psychological test to see if we had what it takes to kill when directed to do so. I tried to tell them what they wanted to hear. There were a number of other written exams, but the one that really got my attention was the language test. They'd created a fictitious language with rules for syntax, grammar and spelling. After reading the rules of this new language, there were several pages of written text to be translated. You can just imagine how the rest of the guys in that room reacted to this one. Each man in the room found something to do with that exam, other than fill it out. Paper airplanes were a popular solution, along with spit-balls and a larger wad for playing circular file basketball. I sat in the back of the room feeling like Charlton Heston at a simian hoedown, and dutifully translated every word.

Now, to be fair, I'd had Latin in school, and in fact had once auditioned to be an altar boy, back in the days when the Catholic Mass still had the dignity and mystery that only Latin could provide. I'd had some French in high school, and a semester of Italian in college. English had been one of my best subjects, and our high school had an excellent English teacher named Stanley Orkis «or Stan the Man, as we called him», so for me, it wasn't so much a test as it was a diversion. That one test changed my life. It got me into Intelligence training, which lead to language school at the Defense Language Institute in Anacostia, Maryland, and to my assignment in Laos. It's amazing to me how your life can sometimes turn on the decisions or the efforts of a single afternoon.

Now I'd arrived in Bangkok on my way to who knew where or what. I was carrying a brown, U.S. State Department diplomatic passport. Only those in charge of getting me to my final destination had a clue as to my actual rank and credentials. My military occupational status read like a secret code itself. Ninety Six Charlie Two Lima Twenty-Seven (96C2L27) meant that I was trained as an interrogator of POWs, qualified as an intelligence analyst and briefer, and had mastered at least one foreign language, in my case, French. I had just arrived from the states on a long flight that began in Oakland, California. We'd landed in Hawaii and later on Guam. We had flown over an intense thunder storm on the way in, and I was intrigued by the sight of lightning which seemed to start in the clouds well below us and hurtled down to earth, below us farther still.

Flying was a relatively new experience for me, having just crossed the country from Atlanta to LA. My parents and I had left Pennsylvania in a heavy January snow storm, and gone south to see my brother's graduation from the U.S. Army helicopter school in Fort Rucker, Alabama. They dropped me at the airport in Atlanta on the way back up North. I flew west to Los Angeles where relatives had picked me up at LAX. I'd never been to the west coast, so it was fun to hang out with my cousins and my uncles in L.A. My cousin, Billy, lent me his street bike while I was in LA. Billy had stayed with my parents when he was stationed in Greenland a few years back. On leave he would work on this Harley he put together from spare parts. I rode cousin Dicky's dirt bike out in the Mojave desert. It was geared so high I could barely keep the front wheel on the ground. My family wanted to show me the sights, so they took me to Disneyland and Knott's Berry Farm, and my uncle took me to my first topless/bottomless bar. No one discussed the war.

Afterwards I flew up to San Francisco and arrived early one morning at the Oakland Army Base in California. I was in a civilian business suit - part of my new collection of threads, courtesy of Uncle Sam. Where I was going the only uniform I ever wore again was completely unmarked. I was scheduled to ship out in a day or two, but had to go through some processing first. Hurry up and wait. It felt odd being out of uniform. The regular army studs didn't like it much, either. I was being issued bedding for my brief stay at Chez Sam, when a young lieutenant wearing quartermaster insignia barked at me, "You better get yourself in a goddamned uniform, boy!" I could tell by the way he said boy with two syllables, he was probably not a northern Yankee like myself, so we weren't going to get along very well. I decided to have a little fun with him, so I whipped out my State Department passport, and proceeded to tell him that he'd better find out just who in the hell he was talking to, before addressing me in that tone. He apologized, addressing me as 'sir', as he either assumed I outranked him, or worse, I was from some branch of government service that only used initials. I was beginning to enjoy my 'undercover' status.

Later that day, I found myself walking into the dayroom to play a little pool and chase away the blues and the boredom. As I entered wearing shades and a dark pin-striped suit, I must have looked pretty odd to the clerk. My black hair was long enough to comb «with sideburns, no less» and I sported a neatly trimmed black mustache. The clerk, a dear little civilian lady in her fifties, blinked and asked in a half whisper, "Can I help you find anyone?" It immediately occurred to me that the clerk had assumed I was CID «Criminal Investigation Division». The nature of her question seemed to imply that she thought I was searching for deserters. In reality, all I was looking for was an empty table, so I responded in a sinister tone, "I'll let you know if I need your help, now get me a table near the door so I can watch who comes and goes." The clerk obliged, excited to think that the game was afoot and she was in on a secret. I remembered a point my uncle, Mario, had made to me on a recent visit to Daytona a few months earlier, "If you walk into a place as if you own it, people will assume that you do." I didn't know what 'my war' was going to be like, or even if I'd survive it. And with the wisdom that only arrogant youth can attain, I started living my life on the principle that if I'm going to die anyway, I'm going to have fun until the music stops.

In no time I was on my way to Thailand. Bangkok was steamy and pungent. I grabbed a cab outside the airport and told the driver to take me to the Capitol Hotel. That was the destination on my orders, and it was an American Army hotel. The cab ride was particularly disorienting in that, like the British, the Thai's drive on what we Americans consider to be the 'wrong side of the road'. Every time the driver passed another vehicle on the right, with oncoming cars, I felt my life span shorten. When I reported in I was greeted by a Sgt. Major who was so anal, that rumor had it that he'd burned the hair off his own head below the 'bowl line', just so that he'd never appear to need a haircut. I can only imagine what he thought of me, now travelling in a sear-sucker suit and looking like something out of a Bogart movie.

Two weeks. That's how long it took them to brief me and to make connections for me to fly up to Vientiane. The Army thought I didn't know where I was going. However, I'd been stationed at Fort Meyer, Virginia, which is adjacent to the Pentagon. There was a Major in my French class who had already been to Laos, and he was headed there again, armed with his new command of French. Most of the senior Lao officer corps, and in fact anyone with a modicum of education there, spoke French. Major Cassidy got me aside one day and said, "I've seen your orders, Bob, and you're not going to Thailand." I'd asked him how he knew, and he told me the code for Laos was on my orders. I walked over to the Pentagon myself, and, sure enough, my orders said "...Thailand, with Duty Station, Project 404." Sometime during the following year the Washington Post did an article exposing Project 404, but at the time the Major pointed it out to me, it was an unknown destination.

In spite of my Top Secret clearance, I had gotten my Dad alone before I left and cryptically told him that if I didn't return, look for my remains in Laos. I made him promise to tell no one, especially my Mom. She was worried enough, with my brother and I both headed to war within two weeks of one another.

My two weeks in Bangkok were not without entertainment. There were delights of a sort to be had by men in Thailand that couldn't be had so readily elsewhere. Bangkok abounded with brothels of all sorts. There wasn't a cab driver in town who couldn't take you to his favorite place. Not that they frequented such establishments, mind you, it was more that they were connected to them. Like tour bus drivers at a gift shop, cabbies received a fee for delivering Americans to these places. The typical scenario was the massage parlor. There were often thirty or more young ladies, each wearing white shorts and a number on her little blue smock. They waited patiently all day on little carpeted steps, akin to bleachers, behind a two-way mirror. Making a choice was difficult because they were all exceedingly beautiful, but once chosen, the little darling would look at you as if to say, "You chose me above all the rest, and for that honor I am grateful." I don't know if it was very honorable, but I do know that it ensured a girl's survival with her employer. A man need only ask the price, and he could take his masseuse home with him for the evening.

After nearly two weeks of briefings and processing by day, and exploring the city by night, I was anxious to get to my real job. One night I decided to go to see the floor show at the NCO club. It was on the ninth floor of a hotel across town. I took my chances in another kami kazee cab, and arrived there around seven in the evening. There was a large cul-de-sac about 30 yards from the entrance to the hotel. It was a typical Bangkok hotel, replete with gecko lizards and insects on the walls all around the lights in early evening, and then later on only the bloated geckos would remain. It was Thailand's answer to the bug light.

There was a floor show band whose first number must have been called 'testing' because that's what the little man kept singing into the mike. I remember a comedian coming out and singing "I hold my pants up with a piece of twine," sung to the tune of "I'll walk the line' by Johnny Cash. It ended with the phrase, "Because you're mine, I'll cut the twine." I was sitting at the bar nursing a scotch, when a British sailor sitting next to me turned and said, "You bloody Yanks!" I said, "Excuse me?" He repeated his greeting and went on to denigrate anything American. Insulted, I pointed out that he was in an American club, drinking American booze, listening to American comedians telling American jokes, and that if it hadn't been for us he'd be speaking German! Scotch will do that to you.

Well, this could only go two ways. Either I'd be slugging it out with a bunch of drunken sailors, or I'd be getting drunk with them. The big guy looked at my face for a moment, and then burst out laughing. We proceeded to order rounds of beer that kept coming for what seems to have been several hours. By the time I got outside it was late, the geckos were stuffed, the insects were all gone (inside the geckos) and most of the cabs were gone as well. I got to the curb of the cul-de-sac, and only then realized that I'd spent all my money trying to keep up with the Brits. I was in a bit of pickle. I needed to get to my hotel across town and was out of money, options and ideas, and had now noticed a pounding in my head akin to hearing one's own pulse through a stethoscope. Being in the dank night air of Bangkok after several hours in the air conditioned deep freeze of the club, only served to make matters worse. I sat on the curb trying to make my head stop pounding and focus on a solution.

I felt a soft little hand gently rest on my shoulder like a fallen leaf. I turned my face up to see a little angel standing over me. She was a lovely child. Her long wispy black hair grazed her face in the warm breeze. Dressed in a loose white blouse, black silk pants and sandals, there was an air about her and a look in her eyes that belied her youthful appearance. This was a child who had seen much. It was hard to tell, but my guess is that she may have been twelve or thirteen years old. She was as fragrant as the cut flowers she sold on a circular wicker tray. The flower girl spoke, "What wrong?" she asked. I told her in language that was less coherent than her own, that I was broke and needed to get back to the Capitol Hotel. She smiled at me as if she were my guardian angel. I never saw where he came from, but somehow there was a cab at my feet, and the little flower girl was talking to him and giving him money. I was aware of being helped into the cab, and my little benefactor was whispering, "You go home now." I watched her as we pulled away, still not sure whether I was dreaming or awake. Bangkok was not a city for an American to be wandering around in broke, and in less than full control of his faculties. She'd done me a real favor.

When I awoke the next morning, I remembered her face. I was so grateful for her kindness that I decided to go back that night and square my debt with her. But that was not to be. My orders came that morning, and I was off on a series of Air America flights that eventually took me over the Mekong and onto the tarmac at Vientiane airport in Laos. I had to put thoughts of my little flower girl aside for now. I had been trying to picture what this place would look like for several months, ever since Maj. Cassidy first told me about my orders. When I'd joined the Army I didn't even know where Vietnam was, and now I was in Laos. I knew it might be the last place I'd live on earth, so I was more than curious as to how it would look and feel.

The odd thing is that I never got it right. First of all, I never counted on the sense of smell being one of the defining factors in my impression of the place. Not that everything smelled bad necessarily, it just smelled different. Laos was also sunnier than I had imagined. I came from Philadelphia, so I knew all about heat and humidity. Philly can be awful in summer. But Laos was so sunny in fact, that it was blindingly bright. The Army flew me up to northern Thailand to a U.S. Air Force base in Udorn. The last leg of my odyssey was flown in an old single engine plane, one of those remarkable acquisitions belonging to Air America, the CIA's private 'airline.' It reeked of fuel and oil. It was a flimsy old crate, with the cylinders all arranged in a circle behind the propeller. It had cheap doors held closed with a simple handle, and opaque plastic windows like an old British sports car. Air America flew anything that would stay in the air. Inside the plane it had been airless and steamy. Outside the plane it was just plain hot. Laos was a tropical incubator.

A black man in his thirties came walking toward me. He was cool looking, nattily dressed, and obviously American. He wore a crisp white shirt with a stylish tie, neatly pressed slacks, and well polished burgundy wing-tipped cordovan shoes. "You must be the new guy," he said, shaking my hand. He was a sharp, self-confident guy, with city élan and a slight southern accent. He introduced himself as a staff Sergeant with DIA «Defense Intelligence Agency», and told me he had a jeep ready to take me to 'the compound'. I asked him my most important question, "Is this a combat zone?" "Oh, yes it is," came the reply. On the ride to the compound I told him I wanted to keep my brother from going to Vietnam. When we arrived at the compound, he set me up with a telephone call that patched me through Hawaii to the Pentagon.

It took about ten minutes to save my brother's life. I had seen the movie about the Sullivan Brothers when I was kid. The five Sullivan Brothers were lost when the ship to which all five were assigned, USS Juneau (CL-52) was sunk on 13 November 1942. Stories of a "Sullivan Act" in connection with family members serving in the same ship or unit are a popular myth. Although proposed after the death of the five Sullivan Brothers, no "Sullivan Act" was ever enacted by Congress related to family members serving together. Similarly, no President has ever issued any executive order forbidding assignment of family members to the same ship or unit. I didn't know whether the law existed or not, but I was pretty sure that Army policy would not favor placing two brothers into a combat zone at the same time. The guy on the other end of the line at the Pentagon assured me that they would change my brother's orders immediately, and they did. I was worried that the two-week delay in Thailand might have meant that my brother already shipped over. I knew it would be harder to get this done if he was already in country and assigned to a unit. My brother never knew why, but his orders were changed just before he was to leave California for the Nam. John called home to say good-bye just before boarding his plane to Indochina. My parents told him that the Pentagon called, and that he was not to get on the plane because his orders had been changed. Apparently more than one man used this as a trick to avoid or delay departure, and the MPs were not buying it. But soon it was confirmed. His unit went to Vietnam without him, and my brother went to Korea. Nixon invaded Cambodia that year. They were shooting helicopters out of the sky with anti-aircraft missiles designed to hit B-52s. It would be like shooting a parakeet with a shotgun. We lost a lot of choppers that year. My parents were relieved. I was elated, and I treasured that little secret until I got home.

Laos was like a wild-west show. I did intelligence briefings every morning and partied at night. I never went anywhere without carrying a concealed weapon. I carried a switchblade knife in my back pocket and wore a pistol in a holster at the small of my back. It was a cut down 410 shotgun, which held one shell in the chamber (with two in my pockets). It had been modified to be held with a pistol grip, and resembled a German Luger. The climate was hot and we all wore our shirts out over our belts to stay cool, so wearing a holster turned on its side worked well to keep the little blunderbuss out of sight. I got to go up into the jungle with some Special Forces buddies now and then, carrying a WWII carbine that had been converted to semi-automatic (an M-2). It could take a 30 round banana clip, and was heavier, but more reliable than an M-16. We flew courier flights with Air America, carrying 'safe-hands' materials «things that couldn't go by radio» to distant field sites up near China and down near Cambodia. Sometimes I flew in C-47s just like the one on the tarmac in the movie, Casablanca. They had twin engines and a little wheel in the back where they rested on their tail. USAID used them for rice drops, among other things. But most of the time I flew in little single engine planes called 'helios'. I guess they got that nickname because they land and take off with very little runway. I was not a pilot but always rode in the co-pilot seat on those trips. We were under direct orders to burn the materials we carried in the event that we were shot down, before leaving the crash site (assuming we'd survived the crash). I carried a concealed weapon on those trips as well.

We were under orders from the American Ambassador himself not to carry weapons in town, but I figured those orders didn't make sense since every enemy we had in Vietnam had an embassy in town along with us. Vientiane was a 'neutral' zone where the enemy came for 'R&R'. It was strange to see guys with communist rifles and insignia shopping at the morning market. You never knew who was on whose side. They had their bars that they frequented, and we had ours. Everyone tried to stay out of each other's way while we were in town. We Americans were supposed to be U.S. AID personnel, not military, so we had to look and act like civilians. It could often be more dangerous for us in town than in the jungle. There were incidents now and then. Somehow, the danger made it seem more exciting.

In retrospect, I am saddened by the thought that what seemed to me an adventure really had larger implications than I realized at the time. I am not proud to admit that I was so uninformed. I reported on the bombing campaign and the 'enemy order of battle', but I really had no concept of what the U.S. was doing to Laos as a country. Since a great portion of the infamous Ho Chi Minh trail ran through Laos, the justification for our bombing campaign lay largely in our efforts to interdict the flow of arms into South Vietnam. However, while I've been home for decades and my part in the war has faded into distant memory, the people of Laos still live with the results of our bombing campaign. We used cluster bombs, horrendous things that burst above ground and send out hundreds of little bomblets to imbed themselves in the ground over a wide area. There are still thousands of these bombs buried in the lands of Laos, and while other international relief agencies have tried for years to address the problem, the U.S. government has done little if anything to even acknowledge its responsibility for having dropped the bombs there in the first place. We were there. We did it. We should fix it. Every year there are incidents of innocent civilians being maimed and killed. The war never ends for them.

Six months into my tour of duty I was due for a little R&R «rest and relaxation» myself. Some guys went to Australia, and although that sounded like fun, I had another agenda. I wanted to go back to Bangkok and find my little flower girl. When my number came up for a break, I took the opportunity to spend the week in Bangkok. I went with a buddy named Arnie. He was a funny guy. We stopped in a big nightclub for a drink, and found that we were the only people in the place. I guess it was too early in the evening. There was a band of young Thai guys up on the stage. I don't know why, but apparently that song was popular back then, because all they sang was 'testing' into the mikes. Arnie and I had one drink each, but when we got up to leave, they brought us a bill that included a charge for a 'floor show'. We both went ballistic, and when we refused to pay the exorbitant bill it looked like we were in for a fight. We were confronted with eight little guys, who looked like extras in a ninja movie. But before any Kung Fu exhibitions could commence, cooler heads prevailed and the manager agreed to adjust the bill. We agreed to pay the drink tab and avoided a potentially ugly incident. As we walked down the sidewalk, Arnie angrily stamped his foot in what turned out to be wet cement. It went all over both of us, so we went back to our hotel to get cleaned up.

Afterward, I went on alone to the hotel to look for the flower girl. No one had seen her. . It had been six months now, and there was no telling where she'd gone. I went back three nights in a row looking for her, but I was having difficulty finding anyone who even knew her. Finally, one cab driver told me that he thought he knew her, and that the girl's mother had been very ill, and that she'd not been around for quite some time. I was disappointed to say the least, but I couldn't shake the feeling that I was going to find her. Then, on the last night before my leave was up, I tried again.

When I stepped from the cab I could hardly believe my eyes. There she was with her little wicker tray, festooned with all manner of brightly colored flowers. They were arranged in a fan-like circle about the tray. I watched her negotiate with an American G.I. for a moment, as I waited unnoticed about ten feet away. When the transaction was completed she was alone again, and she busied herself with the arrangement once more. As I approached her she automatically asked, "You want to buy flower?" She wasn't paying much attention to me, as she tried to show me various individual flowers that might induce a sale. I asked her how much for everything on the tray? She said, "You crazy!" I asked again, "How much for everything – the tray, too?" She rolled her eyes up and to the left, as if there were an adding machine above her on that side. She quoted me a price and I immediately counted out the appropriate amount and handed it to her. She looked at my hands and received the money as if it were an uncontrollable reflex. Then she looked at me briefly but said nothing, as if trying to comprehend what was happening. She handed me the entire tray of flowers. I held it up to my nose and breathed in the confusing aroma of a wide variety of flora, paused, smiled and handed it back to her. I said, "I bought this for you. It's a present. You understand, present?" "You keep, now", I said, "you sell again." I had her going now. Obviously I was a mental case.

I said, "Do you remember me?" I explained to her that she had helped me when I was really in a bad way, and that I'd come to repay her. A slowly dawning light of recognition began to shine in her eyes. Now she proceeded to babble. She explained how her mother had been ill, and that she'd not been able to come to work, and that they were low on money now. She had to work tonight because they were completely broke, but she was worried about leaving her mother alone. I was overjoyed at having found her, and especially pleased that it was at a time when she needed me. But what happened next, was a surprise to us both.

I had known quite a few North Vietnamese who'd been expatriated for religious reasons when the communists took over. They were mostly Catholics and some Buddhists. They lived in Vientiane, and some of the ladies had taken to us Americans. We were occasionally briefed by the CIA station chief to avoid these women, as they might be spies. That from a man who called them "VietManese." We didn't worry much about it. They were often lovely and intelligent women. They had little interest in politics, and were much more concerned with everyday personal survival. I'd met one named Lily. She didn't speak English, only French. She was about thirty years old. We'd really taken a liking to each other, and I even lived with her for a while. Her fractured French was not much different than the broken English we heard everywhere. She'd told me we would lose this war, not because the North Vietnamese were stronger, but because they knew what they were fighting for, and we didn't. We'd stopped seeing each other, but before we broke up Lily had given me a little Buddhist symbol on a gold chain, which I now wore constantly. When In Rome..., I figured. It had been visible through my partially unbuttoned shirt, and the flower girl had focused her now misty eyes on it.

The girl, herself a petite and fragrant flower, had taken my little symbol in her hand and had begun to cry. She looked at me as she allowed the icon to rest gently in her hand, and asked in language easy enough to understand, if I knew what it meant. I told her that it had been given to me by a friend, but that all I knew was that it had something to do with the Buddha. The little girl struggled to explain that there are many Buddhist symbols, each with their own significance. I admired her efforts but spoke no Thai, other than hello. She was getting frustrated and spoke through an emotion choked voice, half laughing and half crying. She was finally able to make me understand that this particular symbol was representative of friends re-uniting. Until that moment, I was unaware that Lily had given it to me in hopes of us getting back together, but now the little talisman had taken on a life of its own.

What had begun as a simple act of kindness in return for an unsolicited favor had become a deeply religious moment for her, and one of the most moving experiences of my life. My eyes welled with tears as I held her in my arms and blinked at the night sky. Stepping back, I looked at her face and touched her cheek with my fingertips. As I gently raised her little face, our eyes made true contact for the first and last time. The silence spoke volumes as we looked through the windows of each other's soul. In a world gone mad, there was a moment of absolute spiritual clarity. Tears flowing down our cheeks, neither of us could speak, and yet what would we have said? No words could have transcended the moment. I lingered, and then, my mission fulfilled, I stepped into a waiting cab and watched her slowly turn away.

What a world this would be if we could all learn to love one another's children. She was a child of that world who taught me about love. I never knew her name. She will forever be, The Flower Girl.

ALEXA

Here I am, let me reach out to hold you
Come to me, let my loving arms enfold you
There's no time, except here and now alone
Where we belong, welcome home.

Many lives, many faces, many freedoms
Many times, many places, many reasons
We survive, and we learn as we go
It's all a game, so welcome home.

There are times when we believe
we know the answers
There are days when we are
spinning, twirling dancers
In our hearts there is room for everyone
If we learn to stand together in the sun

JULIE CRAIG

𝒪 am currently a mother of 2 small children and owner/operator of a small cleaning business. I did not graduate high school, and have no real college education to speak of, to date. At 17, I did place myself in a government run residential at-risk youth program, and I graduated after 10 months with a certificate in Clerical Skills, and my GED. Interestingly, I passed the GED without problem, despite having no formal high school education. I scored exceptionally high marks in reading/writing/comprehension areas. I squeeked by somehow on the math. I have worked using basically menial tasks up to this point, and have ever kept a bright Spirit.

In this moment, tides are changing within me and without at quickened pace. I enter my next phase of my life, where I am called to serve my highest purposes, and I am answering that call. Blessings.

MY PAST LIFE

O was asked to write the story of my life. As I sit today, I am 36 years old, closing in on 37. Some would say I am going more on 50, which I can't say I disagree. I find myself strongly attracted and connected at this age range. Some, like myself, may say at this moment I am going on 13 as well. This, too, I cannot disagree with. 13 is the age life officially changed in drastic ways for me, yet, in eloquently predictable ways as well. 13 is also the age of the last time, until now, I really felt freedom of my soul. I reconnect. 36 is the year of life I officially reclaim and integrate, as a matter of consciousness, the 23 years that have been lived in between, as well as the 13 years lived prior. I begin in today.

In this moment, in the Autumn of 2012, I am newly and freshly moved out of my family home, away from my husband of 6 years. I find myself and my two small children with open luggage cases on the floor of a friends bedroom that has been offered us, and a full storage unit of household belongings awaiting their newly assigned destination. The decision to leave the marriage and change the family dynamic came hard won. I fought the truth at every turn, for 4 years of the relatively short marriage. This could not be. The marriage could be fixed, corrected, just give it enough effort, do my part, see it through. Find the way, MAKE the way. The lessons I have learned through the marriage, and from all of my relationships, have been many. At this point, I see a common thread. A common denominator that I, myself, agreed to take on, very early in life, and have cast unto myself. Until now.

I digress to my beginnings. I was born in a town so small there was no hospital nearby, so my family drove an hour «I may be incorrect on time» to the nearest hospital where I would be born. I was born in the dead of Winter, the only baby in the hospital. My mother was alone during labor with me, no family or staff by her side. A nurse came in periodically to check on her a little, that is what she had by way of support, from my understandings. My mother and I, along with God and Mother Nature, entered into our sacred phase of Birth/Birthing, alone, and together. As a mother now myself, I honor my Mother's strength of Spirit, in so very many ways I may never would have otherwise. Looking on the birth now, it too is eloquent, suiting to my Mother and I's relationship to come.

Early on in life, I felt awkward. Misplaced. Off, somehow. Outside. Looking in. Watching, more than taking part. Waiting for approval, feeling "different". This is how I felt inside. I carried with me a sense of "less than". I took it everywhere I went. It hung on me like drapery, like stench, like a big flashing neon sign. "I hate myself. I am less than you. I am not worthy. I will do anything you want or need, if you'll just please accept, value, and cherish me. Tell me and show me I am worth something." Indeed, that is the basis behind the story of my life, up until now. The feeling of separateness and isolation, of not being good enough for anything or anyone, feeling unworthy of positive interaction, yet craving these things ravagely with all of my soul, is a feeling I have no memory of being without. I seem to have understood how utterly unworthy I was of anything good, by the age of 3. Definitely by age 5.

This experience is less a testament to a sad, poor life, as it is to a beauty of Light, and to a humbling experience of forgiveness. Forgiveness of others, and forgiveness of self. Those good graces came not before many long years of self-inflicted beating, both figurative and literal.

Not only did I feel out casted from the start, I was also pretty smart it seemed. I had a knack for language and comprehension, and a knack for seeing an opportunity in any given situation as well. I could quickly see and pick up on the weak spot in a room or scenario, and often acted on that information for my own benefit. Very early on, by 7 or so, these skills were being used for continual, mostly successful, acts of theft, and fairly skilled lying, story telling, and dare I say, when called for, manipulation of emotion. A few members of my immediate family coined me, "The little actress." This was said in a manner meant as a taunt and degradation, which only lended to more of the same behavior and worse, naturally. What I see now, is how true it was, and how very talented I was. The show of emotions my family members were referring to when they used this slander, were quite genuine, valid and legitimate, and fairly required attention and care at that time. However, the name suits still in another way, and they knew this too, as I was also well known as "Liar" in our household. I really was a great and skilled actress. Oh how I imagined. How I really could put it on. I made up a whole other self, multiple other selves, other lives, another me. I detached from the truth of my current reality in these ways. I made up something else, something different, mostly when speaking to friends. I'd lie till the cows came home about me and my life and experiences. I'd lie about anything, just to make something up that might be exciting or acceptable. My friends knew I was a liar too. Perhaps I wasn't so good after all. Perhaps it was that big, blinking neon sign above my head giving me away. Either way, I eventually and thankfully got over my need for storytelling to the sake of feeling accepted, but I was well in to my early adulthood before that game fell to the wayside.

These skills of dethatching and make believing served me well to see me through my early childhood, though it also made for many blank spaces in my memory. I work to accept and retrieve my memories now. The story telling, lying, make believing and fantasizing, are all testament to an actively creative mind I believe, and to a strong will of Spirit to survive. Those methods also served to get me in more trouble than I can count over the years. The older I got, the bigger and more real the trouble from the stories got.

The first time I recall being caught stealing, I was maybe 7, and I had stolen a full grown woman black (red?) bra from the department store. I wanted to be grown extremely early on as well, from birth probably. I don't recall how I pulled this off, I was truly such a skilled thief there's no telling, but upon arriving home, I slipped it in to a bag of shoes someone had donated to my mother, very pleased with myself for figuring she would simply assume it was part of the donation. Home free! Master plan! I would then have my bra and I would soon be a woman! My mother, being the savvy woman that she is, and knowing me the way she did as well, immediately knew the bra did not belong there when she saw it. When we are children, we don't think of things logically like a grown up may. Simple things, like the tags were probably still on the bra, and we had just been to that store that day, and that my mother probably had seen what was in the bag already, and knew the bra was a new addition. Regardless, I still think it was a pretty good plan for a 7 year old. I was busted, no question as to who could have put the bra there or why or how, it was instantly known to be me, no real questions asked. I was "The One" to go to with these household mysteries. I was the answer to the questions. My mother took me to return it to the manager, and I don't recall much else from that. I was found out thieving a few more times in this time period. Stolen collector coins from my fathers dresser giddily spent down the road at the candy counter. Stolen coins from my uncle's change jar, to the tune of perhaps $25 in coin, who knows. I strategically got them handful by handful each time we went to my Grandmother's house, to pay for little extras I may want on our family road trip to Kansas. Again, my child brain not factoring that my parents and siblings would see me purchasing items and ask about the money, and the items. Again, I still think it was a fairly good and pure of heart plan for a 7 year old.

I didn't get caught much after that period. I stole pretty consistently, anything I wanted, candy and junk food mostly. I felt deprived at home, so I took. I took matters in to my own hands and made my wishes happen on my own. Maybe another testament to the nature of my spirit. Rebellious and righteous, yes, and resourceful. I stole odds and ends and when I became a teenager and the natural evolution to drug/alcohol/cigarette user, I stole mostly those items, and clothing. Mostly from stores, not so much from people, I had somewhat of a rule about that, although I am not entirely innocent of helping myself to others small belongings here and there, which I, myself, deemed as expendable and minor to their world. I have carried something with me all throughout my life. A certain sense of integrity and character, right from wrong, was gifted to me. Perhaps I did learn a thing or two from the belt after all, or from church, or from example. Probably all of the above. Regardless, that part of my upbringing took, enough to see me safely through the dark years. I've been grateful for that precious gift of Light many days, and on many occasions others in the dark places would comment, "What are you doing here? You are a breath of fresh air. You don't belong here. People around here aren't like you," and the like. I always enjoyed this when it came up, and I felt a sense of BRINGING Light to these people and these places, even if only in some small way. I would smile, and say, "Thank you." In spite of my many varied, youthful indiscressions, I can say with a certain sense of odd pride, that I have never stolen items of big value from another human individual for my own ends, I never became physically addicted to any of the drugs or alcohol, by the sheer grace of miracle alone. I will honestly say I have taken on occassion actual cash, and never more than a $50 bill, «or was that a $100 bill?..», and few and far between. Honor amongst thieves I suppose, and amongst "the people". My thinking was more "damn the man" and the stores. I never graduated to bigger crimes related to thievery, or any criminal profession for that matter, though I know with confident, prideful certainty, I would have, and still would be, quite talented in the professional thief trade. Also, I've tossed up ninja, and investigator. Outcast kids are not without many talents.

I entered my teenage years fast and furious. Literally. I hit the ground running the minute I caught the scent of freedom. I felt free. I felt I could stand up for myself, I felt I could fight back. I loved my new independence. I felt independence from my family, and with my supposed friends. I was a new me at 13. I had felt under thumb and kicked around and finally big enough to say "NO!!" And that is what I did. Loudly, and with certainty. I was rebellious, and I was trouble. I basically did what I wanted, when I wanted, and needless to say was out of the family home by the tender young age of 14. I sensed my parents fear. They knew what was upon them, of this I am fairly certain, and my mother let me go quite instantly, after some efforts at institutionalization. At the varied institutions I experienced as a teen, I gained three things; a deeper knowledge of drug use and crime, friends to use with, and introduction to the 12 Steps. I did enjoy the 12 Step meetings. I felt I got good things out of them every time. Nevertheless, it was easier to stick with what was comfortable and familiar, although I appreciated the meetings, and still do. I used drugs fairly heavily and consistently for the next 15 years, alcohol 25. I was very young and mostly on my own, so schooling was over basically at high school start, nobody was around to tell me I had to go. I did have some family members and a boyfriends mother open their home to me here and there, and for them I am eternally grateful for offering their hand. Without them, there is no telling what my story may be. I thank them in this moment. I was a hellion in the end, and ultimately, more than any of them needed to take on. I just wanted to get messed up, that was all I really cared about. Life revolved around getting messed up from age 15 on. Every day, didn't really matter on what.

Life went on this way throughout my teens and 20s. These years were littered with many trials, pains, good and bad memories and friends, many lost pregnancies, boyfriends, abuse, homelessness, chaos, ups and downs. I lived in cars, shelters, motels, hostels, occasionally outside, and with friends. I would sometimes get a place of my own with a boyfriend, only to lose it soon after to the chaos of my unstable drug/alcohol/mental health life cycle I was in the throws of. Everyone around me was just as screwed up inside as I was, in one way or another. Most of us just got worse and worse over time, and some of us got out. All of us were medicating. All of us were looking for our way out, looking for company in our misery, and for a way for us to let ourselves enjoy ourselves for once. The trick as most know, is that this strategy backfires, in the end, nothing but trouble awaits us. The longer we stay in this place, the worse the consequences seem to get. It worked that way for me anyway.

I remember when I hit what I will call my rock bottom. I was 23 and homeless in a place I barely knew after being dumped by my new boyfriend after he saw how needy and off base I really was operating inside, not that he was an inch better. I was as depressed as I ever had been, I mean real bad. Luckily, at the time I did have an old 70's travel van, so at least I had a place for my belongings and a place to lay my head. I drank. I used heavy drugs. I drank and used drugs from the moment of wake up, to pass out, every single day for 3 straight months. I think that's officially called a "bender". During this time I stayed in the slums part of the town I was in, next to the free food bank, and where a tiny little apartment complex happened to be. This complex was chock full of people just like me, doing exactly what I was doing, every single day, all day. I attracted a boyfriend in there, lucky me. I had just been dumped from someone whom, of course, I thought I loved and loved me, I was in a place I did not know well at all, I had no idea what my plan was or where I was going from there, my van needed work, and I had no job, not that I ever held one anyway. Funny how we find our way to our vices though. Funny.. Anyhow, a new relationship kindled. A relationship build purely out of mutual drug and alcohol use, and mutual emotional and mental unstability, as all of my relationships have been up to now. How could I have attracted anything but. I simply couldn't have.

Rock bottom came during this period. I had nothing going for me whatsoever, and I was confused and depressed and wallowing as ever. This new man, quite the charmer, wound up quickly being the most physically abusive man I've ever experienced. I give my thanks to this day that I am still here to tell the tale. We stayed wildly together for 3 years. I think he strangled me the first time within 2 months of our relationship starting, and over me having an open conversation with the male neighbor. More importantly, I allowed it. I accepted it. I let this behavior and treatment go on. That is not to say I enjoyed it, or liked it, or approved of it, in the least. I allowed it, and I accepted it. A green light said, "Go ahead, I don't care about myself. I am garbage. You'll tell me why I deserve to be hurt, and I will fix it." That bright neon sight above my head again. This was my rock bottom. I was strangled to passing out consistently every week for 3 years. No exaggeration. Nothing was good enough to make it stop, and his behavior was truly terrifying. I stayed in that. After so long of becoming what he told me I needed to be for our happiness to stay, and the cycle continuing regardless of anything I ever did or said, or didn't do and didn't say, that beautiful, resourceful, rebellious, strong spirit of mine stood up, and said "NOPE." I stood amazed at myself, at how far I had gone down in my life. I asked myself the first of many vital questions eventually to follow; at that time I said to myself, "Julie, what is wrong with ME that I would stay in something like this, and accept this for myself??! What is wrong with ME here?" That was the very beginning of the end of my legacy of self loathing and varied assaults upon myself. A long new journey back to myself had there begun.

TRANSFORMATION

I finally cooperated with authorities and agreed to press charges on this person, something I had never been able to bring myself to do before this period. I felt a little scared over my feelings cutting it off like that, and staying was so much scarier. I honored the restraining order, and he was placed on a 6 month sentence in jail. Enough time away for me to get clear and start fresh. I stayed with my father for a couple of months and did some much needed journaling. I got a decent enough job and managed to stay working longer than I ever had held a job prior. Progress was happening. I got an apartment with a couple of co-workers and life basically leveled off there the next few years. I had a pretty strong drinking problem at this point in my life, and was still very much battling with strong and heavy emotional/cognitive dysfunction, but I had been clean from drugs for quite a while. I soon saddled up with a young man that crossed my path, as my need for affection and companionship was as strong as any other force in my life. I HAD to have a man, to feel ok, wanted, necessary, desired, beautiful, worthy, physically satisfied. I expressed so much of my internal world and self through sexual contact. I believe now perhaps this is simply the way and an aspect of sexual communion. I chummed around with this young kid, 9 years my junior, as we both used each other for our respective band aid needs. Our relationship was nothing more, nothing less. To be honest, it was nice to have someone there to hold me and laugh with me and be there while I healed, and not have too much emotional commitment there. The arrangement did get tricky after some time however, as the potential there may point to. While I healed and had my companionship needs met, I slowly got myself together, more and more, very little by very little. I slowly began to drink a little less and a little less. I began to focus on eliminating cigarettes. I enrolled in therapy and basically just talked a lot, while she nodded and handed me books from time to time, which I never read. I journaled. I stayed in close touch with my father. I worked consistently and paid my bills responsibly. I was feeling less and less strange, and more and more ok.. little by little, day by day over time.

Looking back now, I can see it was the SMALL, tiny little changes, that made the most effect. It was the little changes I made and consistently kept up with, that kept the ball rolling toward health and wellness. Drinking plenty of water, watching diet, slowing the alcohol, talking positive to myself, being around people I felt good around. Small things in these ways. I genuinely feel those small baby steps are the important steps that saved me, and ultimately would change my life. Maybe this was just me doing my part, while God did His/Hers. Little by little life looked up for me. I took more and more responsibility for myself, my behavior, and my life. I was feeling fairly good and proud of myself. I started a cleaning business at this time which I named "Happy Days Cleaning Service." I chose this as my business name because those were the happiest days of my life to that point. I was feeling relief. Things were definitely happening for me. I still drank and smoked, I still had head and heart issues, I still struggled quite a bit, but less and less all the time.

Suddenly, MUCH to my unsuspecting surprise, I found myself with child. I took the home pregnancy test, and my jaw just dropped. My young lover friend's eyes gleamed and a sly smile crept across his face as I looked up at him, just as mine drew down.. In that moment, he said to me, "Now you're stuck with me", as if more to say, "I've got you!" This was not someone I chose to have child with, so it was not a joyous moment for me that way. I let it be at that, and went about my days. When it was clear this baby was staying put and really coming to the world, about 5 months in, I decided it was really happening and was time to get ready for her appearance. I called up mom 3 states away and asked to come home for awhile, to birth the baby and begin motherhood. My mother said yes and I packed up and moved, and spent the rest of my pregnancy in Utah. By then I loved the daughter growing in my belly and I sang to her and talked to her and "rocked her" in my belly. She was for me. It was clear already that her biological father was not capable of being the kind of father I would require of him, so it was fairly understood that this child was mine, she was for me.

Along came Dakota Rosemary and I had someone to travel

the world with. She is my precious guiding angel, and this human being came to me to help solidify the new life that was budding for me. I was ready for her and she came, in perfect, exquisite time. I have no doubts this girl knew exactly what she was doing when she came to me. She is 7 1/2 now. Here is to a wonderful life together, and to her own precious, magical, and beautiful flight!

The arrival of Dakota truly made solid the changes I was leaning toward in my life. I felt only one thing; to give Dakota the best, most stable life I could ever offer her. This was my only end, my every move and decision I made revolved around this, my number one motivator. Dakota had to be provided with the best environment and opportunity. MY LIFE CHANGED, right then, right there. She came first, my focus was solely on caring for her, providing for her, and enjoying her. My drive to offer her the best life I could and offer her the healthiest environment and mother I could, made things move more quickly in my world. I was plugging along nicely. I was living in government subsidized housing minding my own business raising my baby daughter, I was enrolled in college and was doing well, I was running my little cleaning business, working part time. I spent all my spare time together with Dakota. I didn't do much away from her. During that time, I would say, "It's Dakota and I against the world." And that is how I felt. Happy in our little bubble of a new life.

The Universe had different plans for us than I had at the time, or more honestly and accurately, the Universe saw fit to bring me an opportunity of choice. A cleaning client had suggested I go on Craigslist to find a babysitter for my daughter, as I had no family or friends around to offer help with her. I had never been to the site. I found a babysitter, and also began exploring around the different areas of the site. I would spend nights reading all the personal ads, in all the different areas, for my own enjoyment. I didn't have television, or a social life. Occasionally I would be inspired to respond in conversational manner to some form of ad, purely in a social, connecting to other humans manner, and I would have brief conversations and answers to my questions or comments, and we would go on. It was fun, and my form of entertainment. I responded to a personal ad of a male looking for a female, with a simple question in regards to his ad. I simply asked if he was still in love with his wife. My reasoning was because he referred to her quite a few times in his ad LOOKING FOR ANOTHER WOMAN. I just thought it was funny, and I would point it out to him. That question was the beginning of 4 months of email communications. The ad had no pictures, so I didn't know what this person looked like, I was just conversing. Conversation progressed, we exchanged photos, and eventually had our first date. We began a whirlwind romance. We met, moved in together, were married, and with child all within the span of a year and a half. We moved quickly. I never saw him coming, I wasn't in the market. Or so I thought.

I believe this man and this relationship were an important step in my transformation and evolution as well. I guess all relationships are. Some seem to have significant meaning though. This one was one of those. Problems progressed as quickly as the romance had, and we soon found ourselves in an up again, down again, back and forth, in and out, love and hate, on and off relationship. This was not something I was in the market for, or where I was steering my life. I felt I had fallen so madly, deeply, and truly in love with this person that I stayed like I never stayed before. I hung as tough as I knew how to hang, I found strength I had no idea I was capable of having, which was nice to know. The energy was also exhausting and aging. Where I was placing my energy and efforts was IN to HIM. My focus was on him, my efforts were toward him, my everything was in him. Getting him back, having him focus on me and our life together again, after he had gone in his heart, was something I spent 4 years putting myself in to, and ultimately to fruitless ends. What I did learn though, was wonderful bits about how to be responsible for my half of any partnership, be it with my children, mother, work relations. I am responsible for what I bring to the interactions. That was cool, and a priceless gain to my life. I learned how I, myself, was pushing him away and causing biological repellent emotions within him. I learned about how I was repeating cycles of abuse in my life, and a little more about how I correct that pattern, and be responsible and vigilant to that end, too. I learned how to dethatch myself from someone else's emotions, and let their emotions be their own, instead of unpacking for them and carrying their load for them. Again, a real attraction killer. I learned further how to love myself. What self love and care really mean. I learned further about boundaries, my boundaries, and found my confidence again to state and maintain them.

As I learned more and more over the 4 year period I worked my marriage the best I knew how, I was repeating old cycles, yes, and I was also getting healthier and healthier by the month. Alcohol had always been a huge part of our relation, and I just slowly cut it out, until it was finally non-existent in my life, FINALLY and Hallelujah. Things began happening for me, doors began opening up, people and guidance began appearing in my life that I chose to listen to. Slowly, through the amazing teachers and ways that just kept showing up for me and still are, I began gaining incredible graces I had sought after for as long as I can recall. Through the teaching wisdom of others who began showing up along my path, I began gaining key components to my personal contentment. The vice-like tension I had carried for near 20 years, located in my jaw, temples, ears, base of my neck, and in my shoulders fell away. The overwhelming, loud, and constant chatter inside my head quieted down and slowed, making room for clear thought. My anger and aggression simmered down considerably, to a level I can manage and work with responsibly. My frazzled nerves and insecurities calmed down. My need to medicate with alcohol subsided. I was working the program that was being placed in my path, accepting every opportunity for healing as it showed up, and mountains began to move. My husband hated every inch and second of everything I was doing, and he made sure that was perfectly, crystal, clear. Luckily I continued on, and in the meantime gained more of myself than I have had since birth, became more of myself, came IN TO myself. I am still on this path, growing every single day, and teaching my small children to do the same. The opportunity for my marriage to take a different path was definitely present; I will say that, it simply didn't. For all the varied reasons, people sometimes go their separate ways. The decision to embrace that marital and familial fate came at the time when it was proper. To continue would be to the detriment of all involved. We had completed our contract. I leave it there.

NOW

*A*s I sit today, in this present moment, I am fresh and new. I am such a newborn baby, with all of my newfound life and happiness. My new connection to my true self, and to my own Higher Power of Source, growing each and every day, being nourished each day. I have been relieved of most of my heaviest burdens I unknowingly, and knowingly, lugged around. I have gained the wisdom, insight, and ability to CHOOSE my life, my emotions, and my experience from my point of "Now". My thanks are eternal, and my awe, ever. Such Power this ability to CHOOSE and CREATE my life, this ability to be present in the now, and handle myself with real Love. Such awesome power.

What will I co-create with it?... What will each of us co-create with this power?...

Blessing upon abundant blessing, to each of us.

Delores Crowell

$\mathcal{B}$orn in the beautiful but frigid north. I followed my dream and went to live in the subtropics of Florida. The tropics of South America called to us. We then moved to the great Northwest.

I published a children book named "A Letter to Trevor" 2008

floradoll@fairpoint.net

BEE-ING

$\mathcal{I}$ have been picking berries this summer for a lady who could not do it all herself. She has a field of raspberries; prolific, sweet, bountiful. She makes jam and sells it to all who appreciate the thoroughly organic processes she engages. She and her husband have worked some 15 years to bring about the wondrous, rich soil for these bushes.

To begin the season of harvesting the raspberries, she took me to her greenhouse, showing me the wasp nest in the rafters. They eat the whiteflies, which eat the leaves of the plants, there-by destroying the plants. So the wasps' nests were well tolerated for they help preserve the life of the greenhouse plants. Then she took me to the raspberry bushes where four different kinds of bees were buzzing about. They are smaller than regular bees. They are pollinating the blossoms to bring on the fruit. All these years I have been avoiding bees, giving them a wide berth. Here they were presented as a valuable species that keep the fruit coming all summer long. Some were mason bees, some were similar to bumble bees but about one-fourth the size. They were everywhere, doing that valuable work they do. The service they were rendering warmed my heart and that day I changed my thinking about bees. Now as I gather berries from the vines and hear their familiar buzz, I realize I have let go of past associations. Instead I find myself saying 'thank you for coming, for the work you do, you are wondrous beings.'

I no longer cringe when I hear the sound of bees close by at my place but instead I am heartened by their presence. They like to come into my studio, looking for places to hibernate and yes they find them. During the summer I like to eat outside as often as possible to remind myself that this is what summer feels like. But then, here come the bees. They are especially insistent if I have any meat with my meal for they are meat-eaters.

Sadly there are fewer bees this summer, sad for the planet, sad for my garden plants.

What I learned this day and so quickly, is that knowledge transforms us if we are open to it.

I needed to pick berries this summer so I could change my mind about bees.

EARLY DAYS

O could hardly believe my ears or my good fortune. Someone had just been remarking on how the Ram was appearing as a frog. I rudely interrupted her to confirm that it was so. She insisted it had been report by several people. My inner thoughts and feelings were clambering - I want it, I want it. And so it came to be.

It was late summer and I was out picking wild blackberries when I saw my first frog. It was as small as my thumb, the daintiest thing you ever saw, a green little jewel sitting among the green leaves, about four feet off the ground. I told the little frog how blackberries make jam and jellies of unparalleled flavor and if the berries were plentiful this year I would make some wine. I chatted away incessantly as if it would disappear into thin air should I run out of ideas.

I would see this same kind of frog on other occasions. Then one day I stopped at a garage sale in the town of Rainier where she had dozens and dozens and dozens of frogs in her yard. Some were a little larger and some were brown. When it was obvious I couldn't take my eyes off the frogs, she took me down to a wet spot on her property where there were even more of them She said it was kind of nice having frogs all over her plants, bushes and flowers. I walked around stunned, speechless, having never heard of such a thing.

The most memorable occasion however, came while I was caregiving in someone's home. She had jumped all over me for some infraction-probably some aspect of the food I had prepared was not to her liking. It's hard to believe now that it affected me to any degree but I went outside after a bit and sat on the back porch to calm myself. I saw a movement to my left and turned to find a little frog looking at me. I reached out my hand and it jumped in. It stayed for some time while I returned to a more tranquil state. . Sometimes I put it on my knee but mostly let it be in my hand. When I felt it was time to get back in the house, I put it on the bushes from whence it came. I silently told it I wanted to see it disappear but I never saw any frogs disappear. God, how fortunate we have been. How fortunate we ever are.

FOOTBALL AS A METAPHORE

FOR OUR LIFE

*T*he game of football can be seen as our own life. There is a ball, a coach an opposing team and your own team members. Then there is a goal line. If this game is our life, the goal line must be the end of our lives. So what is going on in this game? We could see it this way: First the player (us) suit up. The principle item in this equipment is a very strong helmet. First and foremost we are protecting our brain. In this game of life, how do we protect our brain as if it is the most important part of our physicality?

(1) We see that it gets prime nutrients for optimum operation.
(2) We do not take in any substance that would kill our brain cells and
(3) We are now aware we are responsible for the development of our own intellect, hence we use the Brain to house the best knowledge out there according to our interests. With this fully operational brain, we are now ready to play the game of life.

We have a coach who has a plan on how to reach the goal line with the vall intact. We believe he can take us into the playoff, he is that good! When the opposition gets tough, he regropes us with a plan to overcome that. This coach can be seen as our accumulated knowledge and experience.

We have a ball «made by the way of a living substance» and we hold this ball close to our chest. There is a ball of energy and light in our chest area. We call it our soul and its job is to record our life. We give attention to this soul so as to arrive at the end of our life with the best recording possible. What are our team players? They are not so much other people, though that could factor in there. Let's call them our intellect, our senses, our intuition «often called our sixth sense». Perhaps too, our inspiration, what inspires us to greatness, to reach the goal line unencumbered with only the ball held close to our Chest.

We are aware there are foul lines where we have been sidetracked into doing things that will not get us to the goal line in the best condition. But we do have a conscious that gets us back on track. And what of the opposing team? They are our attitudes: doubt, fear, guilt, lack are a few of these. But getting back up, resilience is an important part of this game of life. We have been taught well by our coach «knowledge and experience» and we carry on, hopefully unerringly.

When we retire these opposing attitudes, we are no longer burdened by the onslaught of that opposing team and we reach the end of our life with a great celebration of our accomplishments with a ticker-tape parade in our honor.

The game3 of lie has been worth the great effort we have put into it. There have even been times when we had that rare opportunity to kick the ball, that is to say, to take a quantum leap forward! To great life, well lived!

SATORA FREE

Satora arrived in this lifetime with a sense of purpose. She was loaded with coffers of emotional baggage and self-sabotaging programs to which, I am sure, she added on her journey! In her younger years, she felt lost until she found her first spiritual workshop at the age of twenty. Realigning with her divine nature and purpose has been her paramount pursuit ever since. Along this journey she learned effective tools to turn her emotional baggage and self-sabotaging programs into fuel for creating and living the life of her dreams, i.e. fulfilling her chosen purpose.

She currently realizes her dream in her work of love. As Quantum Energetic Realignment facilitator, she assists others to effectively clear up emotional baggage and self-sabotaging programs and realign with their divine expression of choice.

Satora started writing in her teens and used this skill in her work as English to German translator. She is now translating progressive concepts and ideas conceived in a state of alignment into the language of words and illustrations to make them available to interested readers.

For more information about these ideas and Quantum Energetic Realignment, visit www.MyQER.com

NewEarth@fairpoint.net

CHANGE

I once sat at the side of a river bold. It was one of consciousness.

I dared not jump into it for fear of moving too far. So I sat in fear.

The river was wild and ferocious, too wild and fast to swim in it.

So it seemed from where I sat on the bank of the river unknown.

I had no idea where it was headed and where I would wash ashore if I were to jump.

I gazed across the river to see the other side.

There, a faint line. Was this the other side?

I stood up and stretched my neck to better see. It was the other side and it beckoned me.

Cross this river wild? No, no, no, I thought, I am not crazy.

Better to step back from this dangerous edge, fear said. Go to where it is safe.

So I retreated three cautious steps, turned and ran, back to my parents' house. A safe place, I sighed.

Here I knew what I had to do.

I forbade myself to ever visit the river again and lived in boredom, my parents' house.

The night last, before cancer took from my children their mother, I saw it again, the river bold, in my dream.

I curse you, river, I bitterly said, you imprisoned me with your wildness in fear.

I sat at the side of a river bold. It was one of consciousness.
Oh, how I feared and hated it. Why was I born close to such a dreadful river? Why was I drawn to visit this dangerous sight? This folly must end at once.
I set out to build a dam, mighty and tall.
Ah, no more river in sight.
But what was this noise? It was the river roaring.
I built a wall, thicker and stronger than the wall of China.
Did I still hear a faint murmur of flow?
A bigger wall I erected, and then a bigger one yet.
But the biggest of all, the wall to end all connection, I was on top of it now to give the finishing touch.
Tired to the bone, I stumbled and fell.
I grasped for help the concrete trough, as it gave and made me, at the base of security, an early grave.

I lay at the side of a river bold. It was one of consciousness.
I was blind with grief. Why? I did not know.
I felt so sad. I was so alone. I knew not where I was.
I asked not questions of purpose. I only felt alone in so much pain.
Why live? No, life, it was not for me. I was too much pain to bear.
So tired, I could not move.
Thirsty, drenched in tears, I lay.
Away from this place, I wanted to leave.
I drifted off into sweet oblivion.
Ah, feel no more. Be no more what I was.
The river splashed in my face a giddy wave.
Did I wake?

I swim in a river bold. It is one of consciousness.
It is the consciousness of joy and exploration.
It is the consciousness of love freely given.
The river is gentle, the river is wild. I feel light.
My heart leaps as I jump and pirouette in and out of the ceaseless stream.

I swim back and forth to either side.
I explore its banks, its depth, its center, its waves, its life.
I swim against its current, back toward the source.
I relax and go with the flow for a while.
I am still.
I lie in the river and sense its pulse.
I become its pulse.
I start to flow, infinite loving waves.
I expand into the ever-flowing stream.
I flow as a river bold.

I am a river bold. I am consciousness of one.
Now I see all in this moment.

A lonely woman sits at the shore. Do I know her?
She looks out on me, her face hidden behind thick glasses of fear.
I beckon her to come.
She backs up three steps and runs away back to where deadly boredom awaits.

A huge dam looms angrily along my shore, wall after wall stretching behind it.
I see through dense layers of hatred a wasted life cemented in fear.

A listless bundle of pain lies at my bank, its essence escaped
such despair.
The form, so strangely familiar to me, it draws me close.
I lovingly splash the tortured face with a giddy wave.
Will she wake?

Now I know all that was in my moment.
A new moment springs and I change.

I am a river bold. I am change in conscious flow.

STATE OF CONSCIOUSNESS

What I do

where I do it

who is with me and who is not

matters in illusion.

What I am

where my attention is

who I reflect to be and who I am not

matters in reality.

ALEXANDRA GALEANO

Alexandra; born in Bogota, Colombia in the year 1974, is a professional in Publicity and Merchandise, which she studied in the University of San Martin; graduated in 2001.

In the year 2006 she decided to move to the United States, currently she is living in Yelm Washington with her two beautiful daughters aged 12 and 13, but she is unable to forget her beloved country that she left behind, where the biggest wealth is the warmth of the people.

Living so far away from my native home in South America have awoken many feelings of melancholy and the difficult loss of my loved ones have inspired me to write these short poems so that my life will leave its indelible mark and to transmit that magic that exists when your soul speaks.

galeanoali@hotmail.com

MOTHER MUSE

I open my eyes and only see a dream

A dream I will soon wake up from

But when I close my eyes I only see the reality of your venture

Absence that kills

Absence that fills

Your enchanting laugh devastates my happiness

You fill my life with joy

Oh great muse

That flows through the door in my heart

Speak to me so I can express the language in my heart

Your life

My life

My only life

Take me by the hand

To be you're life

I want your forgiveness

You're pride can outwit your feelings

And you prefer to die with pride

Sooner than showing your true colors

Thank you...

It's OK I will run off

Some place far from here

But regret will soon come

All roads lead to you

But now I know the plan

And nothing can tarnish the grateful dead

Love that I feel for you

One day me

One day you

One day us

Until we do.

Dear Mother

My angel who will forever

Dwell in my heart

Do not go

Do not leave me
Drowned in my grief

Always linger in my heart.

LOST

On this the illuminated night

As the majesty of you my leading light

Shining on the steps of my bewildered soul.

ABSENCE

My soul in tears on those long nights

Trapped within me a desperate print

You gentle moon, you 're gentle night in company of kind beings

That would bring me peace

Seal my faith expose my soul

Light the road to knowledge and wisdom.

DEPARTURE

You left with no occasion

Without time to understand that everything has an end

Days, months, years then you're gone

I'm condemned to feel this void

That will only heal when we see each other again.

QUESTIONS

Since you're always on my mind

My heart bleeds and cries in absence

I need to seal pain

Not to feel that you will never return here.

UNDERSTOOD

To love?

What is love?

Not everything you want can be acquired

And the absurd idea of love

Leads you to lose the path

Of who I really want to be

To feel?

How is it to feel?

How not to feel this grief?

Only time will tell

And if I don't feel

I will die thinking of you.

SADNESS

Gloomy loneliness that chokes me

Tying up my arms and feet

Sends me down a rabbit hole

Unable to find myself in whom I really am.

Why cry?

Why tears?

They are the best expression your soul

It's the only way to know that they are symbiotic

And come from the same place.

you

My longing eyes reflect

Your absence and forget

Forever you will remain

In my heart

WHO ARE YOU?

Splendorous brilliant light

Sneaking through the window

Who are you?

Could you be the moon?

DEAF

Do not be deaf

And let your soul speak

Sit silent in the night

and hear what it has to say

Perhaps

you find what makes it hurt

ABYSS ---- 0 ---- SILENCE

Do not hush!

Silence that kills and disturbs

And drags you down

to the madness abyss

ETERNITY

The magic of two lost souls

Consist of being united

by the necessity

That one has to feed on the other

To live for all eternity

COMPLEMENT

Wait for me as the day

waits for the night

As the rocks from the sea wait

for the waves to break against them

Your fight not to wait for me it's inevitable

Because

we are the complement of happiness

BRAVE

Brave

that who lives and breathes

after seeing

the battle is lost

SWEET LONELINESS

Dwell within me

sweet loneliness

Since I don't have

a remedy to avoid you

FARAWAY

I left far away from you,

my love knowing

that I could lose you

now my unreachable

fight to win you back

will make my love for you

to lost forever

SWEET DREAMS

*S*weet dreams

which comfort

my agitated soul

SWEET MUSE

Oh sweet muse of the night

Entering through the gates of my heart

To speak from the deepest of my self

Expressing like this

The best language to enter into your soul

INSPIRATION

My soul mad of inspiration

Wants to extend

my best feelings to your heart

ABSENCE

Absence that kills

Absence that disturbs

Only oblivion will make

this void to go away

THERE ONCE WAS

Every story begins with "Once upon a time" right?? Well, I want to start this one with "There once was" with the hopes that this story will not turn out to be one of those books you pick up, read the first few lines of then snap shut: missing the end of a story I cannot yet conclude; this is why I chose to start it with "there once was".

There once was the power to convey messages to people in the most spectacular manner that has unfortunately been lost due to our minds being lost to all the new technology such as phones, iPads, computers, iPods... Every day, these things distance us more and more from the things that matter.. Our true feelings, being with our loved ones.

We only regret this when it is far too late, when all the words you didn't say *are* left unsaid, when someone dear to you dies.

Today my dead mother made me realize that nothing is forever; that everything has an end and so we should take advantage of the present because that's what it is: a gift, that we should always speak our true feelings, and not postpone what we could do today for tomorrow, because there might not be a tomorrow. I had to live this myself to know it was true, realizing all this time the things we'd been postponing the truly important things, this is why I would like to share this with you: so you can take advantage that your loved ones are around because one day they won't be.

 Do things, say things when you can, show your affection without fearing so you won't have to think back with that painful "would have" "should have" and the empty hollowness that can never be filled.

Ron Harvey

Aka Father Christmas for the Yelm WA community.

D graduated in the late 70's from Dawson Collage with 1 year in Fine Arts and 3 years of Commercial and Graphic Arts training.

From 1978 to 1990, I was in charge of all creation, production and reproduction of Audio Visual support material for both teachers and administration of the Laurenvale School Board's 22 Primary and Secondary schools.

1977 to 1984 I served on the Board of Administration as President for the International Programs in a Community YMCA.

In 1988 - 90, I sat as Vice president on the board for a Company I helped form to assist Immigrants and refugees settle in the community.

During this time, I traveled to Africa, India & Haiti.

In addition, in 1988, I created my own graphics company, 'Creatron' specializing in Logos and letterheads.

From 1985 - 1991, I taught both privately and with the Adult Education Program for the Laurenvale Board Cartooning and Watercolor classes.

1992- Moved to Yelm WA to enroll as a student in Ramtha's School of Enlightenment

1994 - , Created PETA (*Potential Enlightenment through Art*) Productions.

1- Visual Art: - Mastering Watercolor, a transparent Medium that allows the light to reflect back to the observer.
Taught cartooning to children, a Medium that is fun while it builds The art of being present and neuro-muscular control.

1995 2- Performing Art: Performed several plays for the Drew Harvey Theater in Yelm WA. Wrote and performed many puppet shows for this community & for the children and parents at Fort Lewis.

2003   Began researching the true life of Saint Nicholas.

It has been a magical journey being a student of the Great Work and I thank Ramtha for inspiring me to write this book with his tale of Saint Nicholas' initiation.

INTRODUCTION

*T*his is a short version of my book soon to be printed.

Through research that spanned over 6 years and counting, I was able to gather information on the life of what the Roman Christian Church referred to as,

'Saint Nicholas'. Then two hundred years later after his so called death renamed him 'Nicholas the Wonder Worker' in order to dismiss the fact that this was the same person and that he had cheated death. I call this story *fictional* because there is little written records that has survived in what I perceive was the cover up of the truth.

I gathered what little information that I could find and with discernment and synchronicity of events I began writing this story. My teacher in 'The Great Work' Ramtha, inspired me with his tale of how Nicholas himself, was initiated by his uncle into the 'Great Work'.

THE FORBIDDEN STORY OF
SANTA/SAINT NICHOLAS

Nicholas was born in 250 AD along the coast of the Mediterranean Sea in the small fishing village of Patara. Situated in a province called Lycia of the land known as Anatolia. Today it is the small country called Turkey.

His father was Theophane and his mother went by the name of Nonna.

His parents were wealthy; his father being a sea merchant had many ships that transported goods all over the Roman Empire.

At times Young Nicholas's mother would accompany his father on some of his business trips and it was during one of those voyages that tragedy struck.

Nicholas was only 5 years old and left at home in the care of a guardian. She was not only the housekeeper but also his nanny when his parents were away on voyages.

His uncle arrived a few days later at Theophane's home to tell Nicolas the sad news of both his parents lost at sea in a storm.

Nicholas' uncle was the master teacher of a temple school called 'Holy Sion' and the bishop of the city called Myra which was a major shipping port.

Now that Nicolas was placed under his uncles care he was told that he would leave Patara and journey with his him and under his guardianship would be tutored at the Holy Sion school.

Two years later, after being taught writing, reading and fundamental math by uncle it was announced that arrangements had been made for the young boy to set sail to the city of Apamea in Persia to study for 7 years under the Master teacher Iamblichus. Then he would return for his initiation into the Great Work.

It was there that Nicholas learned how to evoke the four elements of nature.

The young boy during his stay befriended a fellow compatriot who would make a tremendous impact in his future life. Her name was Befany and they both studied together in the Great Work in Apamea.

Upon his return voyage Nicholas created his first so called 'Miracle'.

The ship encountered a great storm and was about to sink after taking in a lot of water. Nicholas applied what he had learned, the sea calmed, and everyone was saved from disaster.

Soon after his arrival, his Uncle put Nicholas to the Great Test. The young boy now 14 years of age was to observe the children in the town of Myra from spring to fall then he was to create a gift for each child that was befitting for that specific child.

On the Eve of the Winter Equinox, which is the longest night of the year. He was to deliver them all the gifts autonomously under darkness. Now back in those days this was not an easy task, for the Roman Centurions patrolled constantly the streets at night and anyone caught, they regard as a thief. Under Roman law, the punishment for thieves was crucifixion.

Nicholas not only succeeded in delivering the gifts despite of a couple of frightful moments, but he surpassed his Uncle's expectation.

His uncle told the boy that he would be traveling now to Egypt to study at the great temple school of Serapis in Alexandria.

Nicholas was overjoyed for he remembered that his parents had once told him of this marvelous place were people from all over the world came for knowledge. Alexandria had not only the largest library in the world but held two of the seven wonders on Earth.

Nicholas absorbed like a sponge the philosophies of the great Master teachers who once taught there. Like Aristotle. Ptolemy, Apollonius of Tyanna, Serapis, and many more.

The lessons in levitation intrigued him the most. Back in Persia, Nicholas and Befany along with several other students had witnessed in wonderment their teacher Iamblichus floating off the ground while in deep meditation.

Another intrigue was that of Bio-location the art of being at one place in one moment then, in another the next.

He spent many days visiting the great Moussion. It was a large museum containing models from the great inventers and philosophers of ancient times. His favorite was the works of Hero. He truly was the father of modern day Pneumatics.

Nicholas was in wonder observing the robots that danced, poured drinks and doors that opened by them.

After his 5-year stay in Alexandria, Nicholas lived two more years studying with the Essenes, also known as the Therapeutae. There village was situated just south of the walled city of Alexandria. It was here that he learned the philosophy of the art of healing and the secrets to immortality.

 On Nicholas' voyage, back to Anatolia he was confronted with yet another great storm. Loaded full of wheat, it made the boat unstable in the high waves, battering and tossing the small vessel. A sailor fell to his death from one of the masts onto the deck. Nicholas joined the men on the deck who were praying for deliverance.

Conjuring up the memories of what he was taught by the Essenes and Iamblichus he knelt by the corpse. Closing his eyes, staying very focused and present. After a short time, he was surprised and shocked by the shouting of all the men on board who were now cheering at the miracle that had taken place .

The dead crewmember was sitting up and the storm had calmed leaving a good head wind to fill the sails.

Nicholas tried to explain to them that it was not he but the Divine that calmed the sea and revived the dead sailor but they just could not understand.

Upon arriving in the port of Mira, the sailors hoisted Nicholas up onto their shoulders and carried him through the city shouting out that he had created a miracle and saved their lives.

Finally, he was able to escape and decided to make his way on foot to the monastery of Sion, which was only a short distance on the hill above the port of Myra..

Nicholas arriving at his uncle's home and was greeted by a group of Bishops. Some he had already met before when they had visited his Uncle in the past.

However, this time there was a solemn look on all their faces as they greeted him.

Bishop Theodore of Ascelon informed him that his beloved Uncle had passed away during his sojourn in Egypt.

Nicholas through his notoriety was to become the new Bishop of Myra.

It was not too long afterward that Nicholas met once again his childhood sweetheart, Befany.

After cleverly providing secretly for her and her two older sisters' dowries, they were married. Thus began his illustrious career as the new and youngest Bishop of Myra. Nicholas and his wife continued giving gifts to children on the winter solstice.

The Roman Emperor Diocletian gave orders to arrest all the Christians in the Empire. Nicholas and his wife were arrested and spent some years in prison.

A few years later, they were released under the rule of the new Emperor, Constantine who sided with this growing powerful movement calling themselves The Roman Christian Church.

It was during his married life in Myra that we hear of many miracles being performed by Nicholas. The more confident he felt within himself the greater the works that he performed.

His most famous was he levitating and appearing to fisherman caught in a storm at sea. While hovering above them, he would calm the raging waters.

Another was when he successfully resurrected three murdered young boys two of which were on their way from a king in Persia to be his students. The older broyher was called Babs and his younger brother was called Atana.

Applying what he had learned from the Great work Nicholas was able to perform many marvelous feats that in the past were deemed as miracles but today are explained through Quantum Physics.

Then there was the one that in order to fulfill a promise he filled the cargo hole of a ship with wheat as it moored in Constantinople.

Nicholas suddenly appears at the Council of Nicea in 325 AD much to the surprise of the large gathering of bishops to defend his friend Bishop Arius who refused to agree to the fables that this new Jewish reform movement created. This powerful group of men would succeed in transforming the Roman Empire with its religious tolerances into the non-fanatical Holy Roman Christian Empire for their political and wealthy gain.

Constantine under pressure from this growing political faction proclaims Roman Christianity the official religion of the Roman Empire.

Despite the correspondence between Nicholas and the other non-Roman Christians to attempt to thwart this growing threat from this new powerful movement, the persecutions begin.

A new law forbidding soothsaying or magic under penalty of crucifixion was now the order.

All non Roman Christians fall under the new title of 'Pagan'.

They began to destroy all the temple schools and libraries of antiquity including the one in Myra, which by now rivaled the Alexandria one with its own copies of the great works of past ages.

They then started to hunt down the great master teachers. The great Neoplatonic Movement -- Hermias, Priscianus, Diogenes, Eulalius, Damaskias, Simplicius and Isidorus, fled to the Far East to escape the persecution of Justinian -- the reign of wisdom closed.

Nicholas along with his wife decided to flee as did all the other great master teachers some went to the far east others to south and still others to the far north were the grip of the new Roman Empire had not yet reached.

It was decided that since the pair were being hunted that they would separate and rejoin in an old Celtic settlement in Germania.

Nicholas went through Espanola with his student Atana. Befany went to Italia with his brother, Babs. Both Nicholas and Befany continued the tradition of gift giving on the 25th were ever they went.

Traveling through the Pyrenees Mountains Nicholas and Atana finally made their way to the Atlantic coast and from the Sea Port village of Iria Flavia procured passage on a trade ship heading for the Netherlands..

Upon reaching the Netherlands, wanting to remain anonymous Nicholas just referred to himself as a merchant from Anatolia. When Atana introduced himself, he did so in Arabic calling himself "Zuarte Piet", meaning a humble adept.

Nicholas and Atana stayed with these beautiful people for several years healing the injured and sick and Nicholas never abandoned the gift giving at Yule time.

It was in this second Christmas that Atana presented a special gift to Nicholas.

He had traded some gems given to him by his father for some cloth from one of the merchant ships that had anchored in then bay. He then secretly fashioned a beautiful red colored hooded cloak he had also traded some local hunters for some Ermine fur, which he sewed onto the cuffs of the long sleeves , around the hood and along the edges of this magnificent cloak. As Atana presented his gift to Nicholas, he told him that not only would it keep him warm but also it is a befitting gown to wear for a being of his stature. Nicholas from that day forward wore that cloak during the long Northern winter nights.

One day a villager came to the dwelling where the Bishop and his student were lodging to inform them that some Monks dressed in black robes had arrived on a ship that sailed from Espanola.

That night , suspecting that it was members of the growing Roman Christian Empire following their trail seeking their whereabouts. Nicholas and Atana slipped out of the village under darkness and headed to Thüringen in Germania where the people were free from Roman rule.

They spent the winter with these great warriors. They were adept horsemen and in the spring, they gave us each a horse. Through his infamy, they gave Nicholas a white horse because they said that in their legends, the god Odin rode a white horse and that he reminded them of him. They followed the Rhine River up to Oettenburg the settlement where they were to meet up with Befany.

A month later Befany arrived and a feast were prepared in honor of their reunion.

They had a lot to exchange about the adventures of their journey.

Befany had a lot of news about what has been happening back in their homeland and sadly tells her husband that the Roman Christian fanatics had begun a march around the Mediterranean systematically destroying all the ancient schools of wisdom and arresting or murdering its teachers. Whole libraries burned down and temples devastated.

Babs also had some bad news, his and Atana's father had died and they must return to Persia straight away.

The next morning before their departure Nicholas instructs the two young men to hide as much of the ancient works of the great philosophers as they can get their hands on before they as well fall prey to this rising wave of fanaticism.

Months passed, then one day they received word that their trail was being followed up the river by those wanting to do them harm so both fled to the enchanted Black Forest were they lived in its center for many years

Civilization began to spread along with the Holy Roman Empire's Great Inquisition. Thus the safety of the great forests boundaries diminished. So Nicholas and Befany made their way northward all the way to what today is Finland.

These Laplanders were a very friendly people and gave them a sleigh that was pulled by reindeer, which could travel much easier on the frozen snow.

They lived among these people for many years. Then fearing once again as the shadow of the Dark Ages spread even to this remote area and for their safety, they were told to take refuge in a hollow mountain further north in the Artic Circle.

So that's were Nicholas and Befany headed with a guide to show them its location.

It was a very cold winter and they were very happy to reach their destination .

The temperature inside this mountain was quite comfortable warmed by hot Sulphur springs.

From here, they both perfected the art of bio-location, remote viewing and levitation skills.

There was also a peculiar attribute to this mountain. When Nicholas was in a tranquil meditation, he was able to hear those that were calling out to him for his assistance.

His wife was convinced that it had to do with the fact that the top of the mountain had a lot of pure quartz in it, which she said, amplify thoughts.

There might be some truth to it for the inhabitants of this region today call this big hill Korvatuntoury - The Big Ear.

Therefore, they made this their home with the assistance of the little folks that came with them from the black forest.

From this place once a year, they would depart to continue their gift giving every Christmas Eve.

Many centuries passed and one day a group of Elves appeared on their doorstep and invited both Nicholas and Befany to come live with them at the North Pole.

They told the couple that they had a secret portal there that would take them to the inner earth. They emphasized that it was just a matter of time before evil men would seek them out and that they would be safe there for no one can enter unless they are invited. Nicholas and his wife heeded their warning and went with them and that's were they live even to this day.

Every year Nicholas returned to the surface and continued the tradition of gift giving secretly at night on Christmas Eve for these northern tribesmen who became later known as the people of Russ or what we call today Russian.

Now when the Dutch from the Netherlands arrived in America in 1626 they brought with them the tradition of gift giving during the Yule time and the legend of Sinter Klaus.

Some how the name Sinter Klaus was misunderstood by the early settlers and they began to call this jolly saint, Santa Claus.

In 1863, Thomas Nast who was a writer and illustrator for Harper magazine company wrote a story called *T'was the Night before Christmas*. This story cemented in the minds of everyone even to this day the legend of Old Saint Nick.

Depicted always wearing his red fur lined suit and delivering gifts on Christmas Eve in his sleigh pulled by Reindeer.

In 1931 and in 1964 Coca Cola Company created the drawings we are most familiar with today of Santa Claus.

Does he still live today? Stories abound of a hollow Earth with a great civilization living there. So, what do you think?

This poem is also an inspiration from my initiation into the 'Great Work'.

A PLACE IN MY BRAIN

There is a place in my brain that I always choose,
 A new personality with an old one to lose.
Now my life is enchanted, never aging or sick,
Youth and great health is the state that I pick..

 I am a magical being and I always have been,
Discovering neighborhoods, my mind has never seen.
Past, present or future for me it's the same,
Traveling on neurons, I make it a game.

...

I can heal others, even those from afar,
With a hint from a spider or a shinning blue star.
A genius I am, using my imaging mind,
And with Quantum Physics, the truth did I find.

I can lift off the ground and soar high above,
Like an eagle, a seagull or a spring morning dove.
I walk thru walls, it's not hard for me,
A locked room I can exit without using a key.

I hold out my hand and lo and behold ,
From the void, there appears a coin made of gold.
My fabulous wealth is beyond all measure,
I manifest all I want and share my great treasure.

The love of God shines from me in all its glory
Now that I've owned my dreadful back story
I'm telepathic, I read minds and remote view,
Biolocation I have mastered and time travel too.

This body I wear was only a loan,
My journey never ends in making known the unknown.
Now nothing can hold me, infinity I roam,
I'm a cosmic explorer, the observer going back home.

*With **love** from your brother in the Great Work, we can do it*
- Ron Harvey

SANAKO I. HURTADO

*W*as born and raised in Venezuela, in the midst of a beautiful family who brought her up in a mixture of hard-core politics, city life, and rural wisdom. Her passion in life is the study and practice of the concepts of God, and the spirit within. For the past five years, she has been eagerly dedicated to the understanding of the unavoidable human relationship and interconnectedness with the divine. During those five years, she attended a major School of Ancient Wisdom in the Pacific Northwest, became certified as a quantum healing regressionist, and she has also been developing her own form of energy healing technique, Quantum Attunement. To this day, she continues with her dedication to incorporate and expand the discoveries of her spiritual journey into her day-to-day life.

Author of "Enchanting Nature of a Troubled Soul", a poems book written by inspiration of Source, Sanako shares many of her insights via her blog: sanako77.blogspot.com

A TEA IN TIME

Alexa looked nervous and pale, as she peeked from behind the curtain at the multitudinous crowd gathered inside the main auditorium of the International Western Conference Center, IWCC. The place was packed, and filled with anticipation; anticipation that she had helped fuel for the past 5 years of her life, and that was now nearing its most critical birth moment. She ran her fingers through her hair, and let out a loud sigh of release; her heart racing in her chest, both with expectation and nervousness by the presence behind her.

As a slender 36 year old brunette, Alexa was filled with a passionate vision of the future that she had never quite understood, but that nevertheless brought her to this very decisive moment in her life. She was also a highly empathic and intuitive person, and little did she know just how close she was to finding out why.

She was the only child of a single mother who, having died but a few years ago, had done everything possible to encourage her daughter to always follow her heart, and to value her own gifts at whatever cost: "You don't follow your own heart, girl, and you will end up regretting it for the rest of your life. You will wonder, 'what if', to the end of your days. And don't let anybody tell you that you are not to do just so!" And so she did, to the best of her abilities, every day of her life.

Her greatest passion in life was life itself, and driven by her unique vision of the future, she had grown up with her head filled with ideas on how to make the world brighter, and greater, in many different ways. Yet, at the core of her ideas, it was children who always played the main role. Alexa was of the thought that the only way to create meaningful, and sustainable change in the world, was by reforming the way the world had been educating kids, as well as, what was being taught to them. She wholeheartedly believed, and knew, that children are the future, the central axis of change of any society, of any country, and of any world.

"You know, Alexa, if it wasn't for you and your visionary ideas, I would not be in this position right now." The soft, and intimate male voice behind her brought her back to the present: backstage of the main auditorium, at the IWCC. He went on saying, "It is as if 5 years ago, when you first came into my office, you somehow decided to turn my life's career upside down, and I allowed you to do so! Some still call me crazy. Even I call myself crazy at times! But if this whole idea really comes to happen, it will not be because of me, it will be because of you. I want you to understand that, Alexa. You know that, right? Sometimes I feel like I am just the hand of fate, like I am being driven by an invisible force that came into my life disguised as you, and I can't do anything about it."

Alexa didn't know whether to feel complimented, or sorry for herself and her boss. She certainly didn't envy his position: all of the political and influential eyes of the world were fixed on him at this very moment, on what he was about to propose. Nevertheless, she knew she was not at her best speaking in front of big crowds, or handling politicians. Finally, Alexa replied, "To each his own, Mr. Meyer. See, my mother used to tell me that everybody has their own inner gifts - something that we are really good at from within our hearts - and that it is our responsibility to elaborate on them, to expand them, and not to try and do something that we are not driven to do, something that goes against our heart. So, the way I see it, this is the perfect situation for both of us: I collaborate within the boundaries of what I love to do, and you get to do the same. You are the politician, not me, nor do I want to be one. Everybody is born with a gift, and your gift is in politics, dealing with people and reaching into their hearts with your words, whether you were bred for it, or not. I followed your career before I came to work for you. I saw your passion. I recognized it as my own, but only in a different form. That's why I made it my goal to come to work for you, and I did. I am proud to work with you Mr. Meyer, and I am proud of the fact that you are finding the strength to do this. I was born with these visions inside of me, and you were born to help present them to the World, and to set the wheel in motion." Alexa finished her statement with a big bright smile, which couldn't quite conceal her lack of sleep from the night before.

They had spent all night making sure that every little detail of the presentation was just as they wanted it.

Mr. Meyer looked at Alexa, and scratched his head. Somehow, the sound of her words did not help to calm down the flock of butterflies that had been messing with his stomach since earlier that morning. He held Alexa in his highest regard, which is why he was always respectful, considerate, and tactful with her. He never displayed any kind of behavior that would disturb their professional, yet honest work relationship, and she did so as well. They could talk to each other openly about their deepest ideas and ideals, and even if they got into arguments, most of the times they managed to get to a common ground; though on occasions they just had to agree to disagree. Yet, here they were, 5 years after the first day Alexa stormed into his office asking for a job, and they were about to witness the reaction to, and the preliminary outcome of their 5 years of dedicated work.

Mr. Meyer was about to unveil a ground shaking proposal to reform the educational system, which had the potential to revolutionize the way the world would look 20 to 30 years in the future. At the core of their proposal was the basic fact that, according to their 5 year long research, and previously gathered studies, about 60% of the information that was being taught to children in schools, was either obsolete or incomplete. Additionally, it failed to help the student better understand things like: who, and/or what are they really made out of; what is their relationship to the force we call God; what is their place in creation and their relationship to it, and at the more basic levels, how can they identify their unique gifts, how can they evaluate and expand on them, and how will they relate to others in society based on this kind of information.

One of their main focuses was the idea of introducing children, at a very young age, to the latest concepts and understandings on subjects like: the observer of quantum physics; the hidden capacities of the human body according to the latest human genome research; the role of the human heart's electromagnetic field in cognitive awareness; the effects, implications and potential applications of sounds and frequencies in the molecular structure of physical bodies, as well as, its effects on DNA; and a host of many more interesting and ground breaking subjects. Needless to say, the list was long. The question of 'What kind of world would we live in, if our children were always intrigued and challenged by the hidden potentials of the new and unexplored?' was the main motto of the proposal. As might be expected, their proposal was being confronted by some harsh reactions from the many conservative and radical groups of politicians, and major corporation leaders around the world, who did not like the idea of change, and thought that the world was just fine the way it was. Security was really tight this day since word about their proposal had leaked to the news 2 months prior to the formal presentation at the IWCC, and threats were the order of the day. Alexa's heart was pounding with anticipation, but also, with a deeper sense of fright that she could not understand yet. Her intuitive side kept telling her that something big and unexpected was about to happen. She feared for Mr. Meyer. He had received a couple of personal threats that sounded very serious, but as he had said, "At this point in the game, Alexa, there is no going back. The ball's rolling, whether we like it or not and there is no stopping from here".

It was about time for Mr. Meyer's turn at the podium, so Alexa decided to go and take her seat. She had a reserved seat on the second row from the front, right on the aisle, and next to the emergency door that would lead her back into the backstage, once Mr. Meyer's presentation was over. The place was completely filled, and hoards of news reporters were standing on the aisles, making it even harder for Alexa to get a clear view of the place. They finally announced Mr. Meyer, and the excitement built up in the room; people were cheering and booing at the same time. It was chaotic and frenzied. Alexa's heart pounding desperately, she knew that something was wrong, but she did not know what. She finally got up from her seat, and her eyes scanned the conference room from side to side, looking for something. Mr. Meyer was coming on stage now, and people were cheering even louder. The lights from the camera flashes were blinding, and Alexa's heart was about to leap out of her throat. And then, for a split second, her heart stopped. She heard a man yelling from the distance: "Coward! Traitor! You can't do this!" Alexa followed the direction of his voice, and then she saw the man: he was about 8 rows back from where she was, and he was forcing his way down through the mass of news reporters who didn't know what was happening. But Alexa was fixed on the man's face, and forcing her way towards him, desperate to reach him before the worst could happen. Her heart was racing, yet it did not cloud the conviction and determination to stop him at all costs. The man was now 2 rows from Alexa. She saw his right hand reach inside his jacket, and caught a glimpse of it grasping metal, "A gun! He's got a gun!" she thought to herself, forcing frantically to try and grab his hand in the midst of her own incredulity with what was happening.

She pushed with all her will, and made her way through the mass of confused audience and news reporters. When she finally got near him, everything was bizarre: a big blob of slow motion and hazy faces, yet all that she could see was the man's left eye. She did not understand why, but she kept looking for eye contact. She yelled at him, but in the midst of the chaos the man didn't seem to hear her words; there were people screaming, news reporters flashing their cameras, security guards flying horizontally in the air attempting to reach the man, as well as others on stage attempting to safe guard Mr. Meyer... it was a zoo gone crazy. Nobody quite understood what was happening, and neither did she, yet, before she even knew it, there she was face to face with the mad man. His gun was now pointing straight at her chest, for she had just gotten in between him and his target. Then, the most strange and unexpected thing happened: He looked at her, right into her left eye, and she looked right into his. She noticed his eye was pale blue, lacking any brilliance, almost white. It was something unusual, yet beautiful, in a weird kind of way. He looked at hers, but hers was a sparkling copper with rays of gold. He thought it looked like a jewel. Then, and at the same time, they both seemed to be sucked into the other's iris; in, and in, and then in, until all around them faded, became dark, and quiet. She could still see the pale blue eye, and he could still see the jewel, but all else was black, like an endless and silent void.

They floated through this endless void for a period of time none could understand, until finally they saw a little light. They each focused on the tiny little light, and followed it. The light grew bigger and bigger, as each drew closer to it, until it eventually enveloped them all around. It was the most pristine, brilliant, sparkling and golden white light they had ever seen. It was breath taking and blinding at first, but then, it became apparent that there was a sense of space within this light. They heard a brief high pitched noise, and turned towards it, only to find themselves facing each other, while sitting on opposite ends of a small, white coffee table. They were still staring into each other's left eye, with nothing more than the small coffee table in between them, and a cup of freshly brewed hot tea in front of each one. The smell was soothing and inviting.

Alexa and the man stared at each other, then looked down at their respective cup of tea, and then back at each other. They were not scared, or startled, but more like, confused and disoriented. They both took their cups, and brought them to their noses, noting with curiosity how it just happened to be their favorite flavor. Alexa finally commented on the situation, "Is this a dream?" The man looked at her puzzled, and then back at the cup of tea he was holding with his right hand, "I don't know" he said, "I was just about to ask you the same question". They tasted their tea, and were surprised to find out that it was just the perfect temperature: not too hot, not to cold, just soothing, comforting and plain delicious.

"Do I know you from somewhere?" asked Alexa.

"Hard to say" responded the man. "There's so many people that I see every day, and they change, they always change."

"Are we dead?" She added.

"I don't think I pulled the trigger, and I don't remember hearing any gun shots" he replied, while slowly and calmly taking another sip of tea.

"Well, me neither. But then again, I don't think that either one of us remember how we even got here in the first place... wherever 'here' is anyways." Alexa said, showing obvious signs of confusion with the whole situation.

"The last thing that I remember is seeing a jewel in front of me, as I got ready to fire" The man added.

"Oh! Yeah! Speaking of which, why did you do it?" Asked Alexa, displaying obvious concern and accusation in her tone, "Do you even understand the importance of what Mr. Meyer is about to propose to this country? To the world?"

The man took another sip of tea, as calmly as ever, then looked back at her and said, "I don't know. Do you?"

Alexa thought she was going to jump at the man, "Of course I do!" she said, "I have been working with him for the past 5 years on this project. Now, I know that he has definitely deviated from the preaching line of his party, but isn't that what we are supposed to be doing?" She said, clearly defying the man to reveal just how ignorant he was of the whole situation.

"Doing what?" he asked

"Changing the world!" she added, "What is the purpose of discovering things, if it is not to redefine our current concepts about life, and the way we go about it?"

"Redefine?" asked the man, "What makes you people think that you can just come and change, or impose on another, what to learn or believe in?" He looked at her showing signs of what appeared to be agitation.

But Alexa went on to say, "Who is talking about believing? We are talking about ground breaking research done by expert scientists all over the world, scientists that are out there saying that things are not quite like we used to think, that the universe seems to work in a much different way than what we used to 'believe'. The implications of information like this relates directly to the way we see, and perceive ourselves individually, and as a whole. It has a major social, economical, religious, moral and cultural impact. And yes, I know, that sounds frightening, but isn't that outlook better than the one where we just live and move by a predetermined set of old, obsolete rules until the end of times? It is no different than when people used to die in hoards, because they had no idea about something called "microbes" that could be easily removed with proper hygiene."

The man looked at her seemingly confused, and puzzled. He shook his head and took another sip of tea, bringing the cup back down with a hard sound over the table. "I don't know" he said shaking his head, "These things that you speak of, I have no idea of them. How do I know that what you are saying is true?"

Alexa looked around them with frustration. The space looked white and pristine as ever. It didn't seem to have walls, but there was no sense of space beyond the area where the two of them sat. "Well for one, while we are stuck here, I cannot show you the material and research that we have been working on for the past five years. And if we were ever to come back from whatever this place is, I doubt you'll get the chance to see the presentation. But trust me when I tell you that the information is out there, for the one with the eyes and the willingness to see it. The only reason that this information is not in the mass media, is precisely because of the kind of reaction it produces in the people that are comfortable with the status quo." Alexa looked at the man's expression not knowing what to make of it. She finally gave out a loud sigh, and said, "Oh! I wish I could just show you. All I can tell you is that the implications of the findings, from many of the greatest scientists in the world, are huge! And it bears asking: if this is what the current generation of scientists are accomplishing right now, with the kinds of barriers imposed on them by the conservative, greedy politicians, and corporations around the world, imagine what the future generations of scientists could do if they were exposed to this information, and supported, at a very young age?" Alexa looked at the man, and could see that he was following her train of thought, so she ventured to continue, saying, "If only but a few of those kids were to develop a strong enough curiosity for some of these subjects, it would mean the furthering of development in those particular areas of research. Imagine what they would be able to build upon: rather than building upon war, disease, tragedy, and any of those repetitions, they'd get to build upon life, brilliance, curiosity, possibilities, hope, unlimited health and true evolution. They would get to accept, and see 'change' as a natural way of living; rather than praising stagnation, and holding a crooked kind of reverence for the old. These would be kids that grow to know that they are worthy by themselves, and not by who they imitate. Imagine what the world would look like, how enriched and changed it would be if we would get to accept, and promote the natural diversity of humanity, and the equal-ness of importance in the expression of that diversity. Everything has a cycle, even ideas, and I know that part of our job is to keep this world expanding, changing, by ever building upon the old to create something new, refreshed, and that can transition each original idea into something greater. Yet instead, the current state of affairs in this world seems to favor a regurgitation of the old ideas; it's like making today's dinner with yesterday's scraps, over, and over, and over again. No wonder the world is in chaos, almost in a self-destructive mode; there is no movement of ideas! Instead of living to give birth to ever new and refreshed ideas, it is like we are trapped inside of a circle, like a dog chasing its tail! The world chases and ostracizes the few ones who dare to explore the new. Can't you see the madness in all of it? Would you not want to get out of this addictive labyrinth, and experience something different?" Alexa asked the man with eyes wide open. In her excitement she even forgot the man was there, it was as if she was talking to herself.

The man looked at her inquisitively: his face was serious, in an obvious state of deep thought. He took another sip of his tea, noticing how it still was just the perfect temperature. "Impressive!" he thought to himself, and then finally looked at Alexa, and asked, "Why do you say it is a labyrinth? And why is it addictive? I don't think I quite follow you on that."

Alexa paused, and bit her lower lip, obviously thinking very intently about the best way to explain her thought processes to the man. She finally said, "Alright, imagine a big labyrinth floating in front of you: The way I see it is that, if you look at the current ways of thinking of the majority of people around the world, as well as, its resulting gamut of ramifications into the way we relate with each other at all levels, you will notice that it is pretty obvious that these current ways of thinking are based on a set of specific, and preconceived concepts and beliefs. And I say preconceived because the earliest impactful episode in history that has altered the ways of thinking, and behaving in the world, it's been the sexual revolution. That revolution has been going on for several decades already, as it started with the occupational and sexual emancipation of women, and later on, with the global and legal acceptance of homosexuality. But besides that, the knowledge that is given in schools, which plays a major role «if not definite» in shaping and defining the course of our lives in society - that knowledge has varied very little in the last 40 years. 40 years! On the other hand, the rate at which our kids can learn has increased about 40% in the last 30 years, and the educational system has done nothing to catch up with that. Instead, we have continued to teach the same, so that as a result, society can continue to be the same. If you look at how fast technology has advanced as well, shouldn't that point directly to what is happening inside our heads? Inside our bodies? Doesn't that at least beg the question?"

She looked at him as if waiting for him to say something, but he didn't. So she continued elaborating, "For as long as we continue to teach the same, our world is like a closed labyrinth, with no entrance or exits, no way out. No wonder they always say that history repeats itself, doesn't that sentence give you a sense of claustrophobia? It repeats itself because we keep teaching the same, along with the same values, same morals, over and over again. It is like taking a monkey and dressing it with different clothes and, because of the different clothes, we want to call it an elephant! It is still the same monkey, but wrapped in a different way. We forget to pass on the idea that our job may be to outgrow our past; but of course, who will say that first, if no one is ever even taught the idea of it? So, in the end, the labyrinth can only be exited vertically, and up. From there on, we go to build another one, greater, bigger, different, and we will exit that one when we have explored each and every corner of it, and have grown bored with it. It is like a never ending, expansive and upward creation process of idea-experience-expansion, and then back again to a new idea. It does not disregard the previous one, for the experience of the one before is the ground upon which we build the next one."

The man looked at her without being able to utter a word. He appeared to be intrigued, and to be taking his time to let all of this information sink in. He nodded with his head, signaling to Alexa that she could continue elaborating, and so she did.

"The reason I say it is addictive is because of our resistance to change. In a way, humans are just as animals; they can be, and are creatures of habit. The thing is, what do you make a habit of? When one does not like change, because it corrupts or compromises our current comfort zone, one will fight to keep the old going no matter how toxic to self or others it may be. This is no different than what addicts do when someone outside of them is attempting to make them quit. They cannot see the need for change, for they just know that it feels really good to do their thing; and most of the time, even though they may be aware of how compromising their habit is, until they have had enough of the whole thing, they won't stop! This is the same for the ones feeling comfortable with what they do, day in, day out: When someone comes along to challenge the status quo, to offer change, even if to improve it, it is usually vehemently rejected out of plain fear of the unknown, because we don't know, or understand how this new change will affect our current state of affairs."

The man was silent. His face had no expression that Alexa could decipher, but he looked intently into her eyes, while grasping his cup of tea very firmly, as if he didn't want to let it drop. Alexa grabbed a hold of her own cup and took a long sip, delighting in its fragrance and perfect temperature. Whatever this place was, they sure made an awesome cup of tea, she thought to herself.

The man stirred in his chair, noticing that he felt light and vibrant. In this place, he always felt youthful, energetic, and filled with the elixir of life itself. He looked at Alexa, and asked, "And what about your politician?"

She looked at him puzzled. He obviously caught her off guard with the question, "What about him?" she asked back.

"What does he really think about this?" he asked, "Is he really game for this? Does he have what it takes? Is he strong enough to carry on with this venture of yours, even with all that is about to come his way after he makes this presentation?"

Alexa took another sip of tea, let out a loud sigh, and then replied "Look, all I can say is that all of my life I have been plagued, you could say, by these ideas of changing the world, but I never knew exactly why, or what to do about it. When I first saw him in the news, there was something about him that struck a chord. I don't know what that is, but my intuition has never failed me. In a way, I just know that I was meant to be a message carrier, and he was to be a delivery agent for this project. From the first time that I met him in person, I knew my intuition was right. I knew that I could trust him with my ideas, and that he would build upon them, and so he did. It's almost as if we were some sort of a pre-arranged work team, and we are only carrying out our parts." She looked at the man, and then continued to add, "He is definitely stronger than what he thinks he is, and for some reason, I think that he will find out very soon just how strong he really is. So, I guess the short version to your answer is, Yes, I do believe he's got what it takes."

He looked at Alexa with no expression in his face, completely neutral and devoid of emotion. He took a long sip of tea, and then added, "That remains to be seen."

She looked at him intrigued, and now her face was turning grave. She could sense a moment of fate was about to come; a turning point in her life was around the corner, and she could feel it now, just as she had felt it many other times throughout her life. Slowly she put her cup back on the table, and took a deep breath, if there was actually any air to breathe in this place. But she gathered herself up, and finally asked the man, "What do you mean by that?"

The man looked at Alexa straight into her eyes. His expression, now softened, revealed a second intent behind his words that she could not make any sense of, at least not quite yet. He kept looking at her intently, as if waiting for her to recognize something about him. As soon as she realized this, her gaze became inquisitive, but she still could not get it. She finally asked him in frustration, "Who are you? I mean, for real. I have a sense that you are not just some random crazy guy running around with a gun, trying to murder people. Who are you? Am I supposed to know you?"

The man's eyes were warm towards Alexa now. He shook his head side to side, and bit his lips almost unable to contain the beginnings of an open smile out of the corner of his mouth. He shook his head again, and said to her, "You really don't know, do you?"

Alexa's mouth and eyes were half way open, studying the man's expression; frustration running through her whole being, from not being able to recognize who this mysterious man really was. She shook her head lightly, and with eyes wide opened expressed, "No! Tell me, what am I missing?"

The man reached across the table, and very gently took her hands in between his. Alexa's eyes got even wider, as she felt a surge of something like electricity run through her being-ness at the mere sense of his touch. There was a sense of deep recognition, but it was not physical, for she doubted they were really physical in this place. He looked deeply into her eyes, his eyes now dark green with rays of gold, Alexa thought to herself those eyes were very familiar. The man moved closer to her face, looked deeper into her eyes, and then she saw it: with a wild expression of disbelief, she let go of his hands, and brought both hands to her mouth in an effort to contain her utter amazement, at the same time. He remained calm next to her, looking into her eyes and quietly smiling.

When she was finally able to speak, she said to him, "You?! How can you? You are Mr. Meyer?! But how? How can that be? I thought you were the man coming to kill him. I don't understand, is this real?" Alexa brought both her hands to her head, in an attempt to calm herself. She felt dizzy, and her whole being was vibrating very fast.

The man took Alexa's cup, and gently put it in her hands inviting her to take a sip. She found it to be soothing, and surprisingly calming to her over excited senses. She felt her eyes were wide open, and as she kept looking straight into the man's eyes, he smiled back at her, and said, "In the terms of your world, you could say that I am a part of Mr. Meyer's higher self, but only a fraction of him, no more than I am also a fraction of you." He looked into her eyes, but she was still lost. "I am what some call, the essence that lies past, or beyond, the firings of the neural nets of his brain... or your brain. I am not bound by physicality, nor can I be encapsulated under one name only. However, to your understanding right at this moment, you could say that I am acting as, and in behalf of the part of us which is called 'Mr. Milton Meyer'. I am that part which observes the propensities of his firings, and is capable of re-organizing it in order to ensure a proper, or different type of experience, more conducive to the over-All goal of re-unification of the Is-ness."

Alexa was still, frozen in place, immersed in a sort of shock and disbelief mode. The man continued adding, "You see me with this physical form because the mad man with the gun was the last person that you saw, right before we brought you to *here*".

"We?" Alexa asked intrigued, finally able to utter a word. "Who is this 'we' that you speak of?"

The man looked at her quietly, like a father looking at his 4 year-old child who is wondering where children come from. He finally said, "I know this seems out of one of your science fiction movies, but I assure you, this is very real. The 'we' that I speak of, is you, me, along with others that we collaborate with. You just can't remember. "

Alexa's mouth was now wide open. She said to the man, "Me? But, I don't see another 'me' here, or these other people that you speak of. Where are they? Where am I?"

"It is not done that way, Alexa" replied the man. "You can only see what, and who will be more conducive to the expansion of your individual experience according to your level of understanding and awareness; and that is decided by yourself, in a manner that I cannot possibly explain to you with words, right now. Your words are extremely limited in their capacity to convey the multiplicity, and complexity of the way things actually are; and even my understanding of it, is still not all-encompassing. It should be enough to say that, this setting, this persona, this manner of encounter has been chosen by you and me for the sake of easing your choice."

Alexa's face became grave at the mere sound of the word 'choice', and there it was again, that weird sensation which preceded any episode in her life where a moment of truth, a turning point was about to happen. She finally dared, and asked, "What choice?"

The man looked at her with warmth in his eyes, and replied, "Whether you are aware of it or not, whether you like it or not, you confabulated to create this very moment. You chose to come here and have this conversation, this moment of seeming choice. In that reality from which both of us have paused, something is about to happen, that may forever change the face of humanity in this particular frame of illusion, this particular permutation of reality. Yet, that possibility, as projected in this moment, can only happen if you were to choose a certain path. The seeming choices that we make, determine a certain path of experience that most like to call 'evolution', which may be collective, or individual, and sometimes even both. Though the joke of it is, that All is One, so it is always collective, and it is always individual. You and I have been together for, what you would term, a long journey of self exploration and understanding, which has taken us on some wild rides throughout the domains of time and space. Yet, never before had we embarked upon the experience of helping a whole frame of reality to shift frequency; which means, the evolution of a whole race, a whole concept of reality that was encapsulated within the denomination of a planetary sub-division of creation. When we came across the opportunity to do so, we thought it would be quite the experience; for the purpose of reunification of the whole into a collective experience, and from there, back into oneness. We have been for some 'time' working, you could say, with a group of other multidimensional beings; entities, who entered this particular frame of illusion at several critical points in 'time', and we are attempting multiple permutations of choices, in our search for the experience of a collective shift in consciousness of this planetary sub-division as a whole. Our personal closeness is very strong, in the midst of the forgetfulness of our original intent; and even though most of the time that closeness has been a source of expansion, in this particular domain of reality, the density of it makes it difficult not want to just stick together. I already supported you once in making the 'hard' choice. Hard, for the conscious personality, for the wirings in your brain which make you think that you are Alexa. Nevertheless, the hardness is very real, and the emotions that accompany it as well. At that time, I helped you because I knew it was the turning point of your experience. So, now I am asking you to remember, and consider to return the favor. Without the 'hard' choice, we estimate that the possibility of expansion, for this particular frame, would require several thousand permutations more, which may translate into some hundreds of years in Earth-linear time. And let's not forget to mention, that it may involve the experience of some hard core cataclysmic events along the way, which are completely unnecessary at this particular moment in the illusion."

Alexa's face was filled with disbelief and confusion. Yet, a deeper part of her knew that, somehow, all of this mumbo jumbo resonated as truth in some far corner of her being; a corner of which she had no conscious awareness, until now. Intuitively, she knew that he was speaking truth, at least to some degree, about the nature of her relationship to Mr. Meyer. The man went on to say, "The turn of the tide has come, Alexa, right now. A change: for you, within the expectations that you might have had for this particular life that you have been living as Alexa; but also for humanity, and for all the entities that have been ceaselessly attempting to finally turn the circle into a spiral, and from there, finally out of it, and into a totally different realm of experience. All of that drive that you have felt for changing the awareness of expression in children: from a system of externalization of reality, into a system of internalization, that will forever bring into true Oneness the human race, when it can finally acknowledge itself in the other; all of that can, and will be achieved. It is just a matter of 'when', and 'how'. There is a chance, right now, right here this moment, for this particular frame of illusion."

Alexa couldn't speak. A volcano of super cold energy was about to explode inside her chest. She became really still, and all of a sudden the bubbling intensified, as waves of multicolored pebbles of energy blasted in and out of her breast plate. With each blast, she would have instant moments of remembrance: She was in space, inside a glowing white ship that seemed to be made entirely out of energy. She was dressed in tight and brilliant white garments, and the man was there as well, smiling, and talking to her. She could feel the warmth of comradeship between them. With another blast she was floating in what seemed to be space. The shape of her body was indescribable, and she saw hoards of squid like glowing entities floating next to her, and then she knew that she was one of them. They were plainly angelic, made out of a soft glowing, milky white energy body. They were moving as one big swarm; basking through space, and emitting an almost inaudible hum that felt like total ecstasy. Thousands of memories flashed back in a matter of just a few moments, as every blast of energy opened more and more her channel of light in the heart. She felt like crying from happiness, yet, tears wouldn't come out, not in this place. When the process finally stopped, Alexa was glowing with the most subtle, and pristine crystalline light. She remembered, though not all of it, but enough to recognize the man, and to know that his story, and her part in it, was true. She remembered that we all are truly One. She was in bliss, and in total awe of the moment. Finally, Alexa asked the man, "So, what happens now? Do I stay here, and die there?"

The man chuckled, and smiled at her, "No, that's not how it's done. At least not this round. Martyrdom is not necessary to accomplish the task. What really matters is that Mr. Meyer would benefit greatly from letting go of the illusion that he needs you in order to accomplish the goal. Without that, the thrust of his energies will never reach its peak potential, for he will always lean on you. Do you understand that?"

"Yes, I completely do" replied Alexa.

"Great," said the man. "You see, you are a sort of a transmitter-receiver device, meaning, that you are designed by higher order to communicate with Source, and bring 'ITS' instructions of experience, all the way back here. You have the power to be a link between the subtle and formless, and the dense realms of time and space. You thrive on it. We are world makers, bringers of ideas. Each piece of the puzzle has a particular pattern and colors to it, and when we deny them, we believe that we are disconnected from Source... or as they call it in this frame, God. The thing of the matter is, we are NEVER disconnected. It is impossible to be disconnected from that which we ultimately are. No matter where we 'go', it follows us, because IT IS us. Each and every one of us, playing and experiencing each level of illusion; and each experience, no matter how hard or easy it seems, it is equally valid, and loved. So, you see, you get to pick your next course of action, based on whether you wish to continue to be a part of the one particular experiment that I have talked to you about, or not. Either way, it really is fine."

Alexa looked at the man with glowing eyes, almost jumping with excitement: She was he, and he was she. She added, "Alright, then what do I get to do? How do I get out of the picture, without you actually firing the gun and killing me? I mean, as far as I remember, the gun is pointing right at my chest."

The man smiled gently, and added, "That is no problem. You will be shot, but you will not die. It will be something minor. However, you must NOT let Mr. Meyer cancel the presentation. He needs to get through it, without you by his side. After you are done recovering from your wound, the flame of your heart will lead you to your next experience. Take some time alone, and rekindle this 'connection' that has happened today. You will receive further information during that time, and you will know where to go, what to do, and who to look for. Do your best to remember as much as possible from what has happened here, for you will lose some of it as your consciousness goes back into the density of your body."

She was quiet, and peaceful. A soft curve adorned the corner of her lips, and she felt like the whole world was inside her chest. She loved every one, she could see every living being, every thought or idea having ever been conceived, into any shape or form. She was all of it. She could hear the laughter, the joy, the sorrow, and the pain of every living soul; but nothing weighed heavy. All of it was absolutely delightful. The state of openness that Alexa was experiencing was so vast and encompassing, that she felt no longer female; no longer human; no longer a differentiated being; no longer a planet, or a galaxy; no longer separated; no longer many...she was all, and all was really one being. She could feel the vibration of every living thought, and it tickled. The energy of all that was, and is: inhaling itself out of existence, and exhaling itself back into existence; the thrust of energy in the form of the sexual act, as the manner in which the All reinserts itself back into a frame of illusion. There was no separation, and no individuality; it was all one big body movement: every laughter, every question, every uttered word, every given step, every sneeze, every birth, and every death. All was fine, and eternal. It was all a big game, and she had remembered her part on it. As she was coming back down into her body, she knew that she would forever remember this place, this state, this being-ness, because that is who she really is. That is who you really are... who we all are.

DR. CORNELIA O'LEARY

*G*rew up in Cork City, Ireland and left her native country aged 25, at the end of her medical internship, to work in the UK. In London's teaching hospitals, she qualified as a pediatrician and anesthesiologist. Her career also included work as a medical advisor to a major multinational pharmaceutical company and the UK Medical Regulatory Agency. In addition, she had her own practice in complimentary medicine for 20 years, specializing in magnetic therapy, which was filmed and shown on prime time mainstream television. Her research into the association of electromagnetic radiation and Sudden Infant Death Syndrome (SIDS), presented in London, was reported in the mainstream press and is referenced by Robert O. Becker in his book, 'The Body Electric'.

Her passion for truth, knowledge and human potential has led her along many avenues of learning and experience and to presently reside on her organic farm in Yelm, Washington, USA. She has never written for non-medical publication before but in December 2008, the words of a poem/song came to her to the beat of a rap and she wrote them down. She called the piece 'Attitude'.

A Rap Poem/Song
«Can be read to the beat of a rap»

ATTITUDE

Subtitle: L & G Rap

I've got an attitude
Of love and gratitude
It's not just a platitude
It's the real thing

Get in the attitude and be in the swing
It's a cool thing
Better than bling

It's real glitter, not to be bitter
In the attitude of gratitude
Bells will ring

Whatever my trouble
I get on the double
With an attitude of gratitude
I can only win
...

...

CHORUS...

I've got an attitude
Of love and gratitude
It's not just a platitude
It's the real thing

Don't diss me now
It'll piss me now
And where is my attitude of gratitude then?

It does no good, to be in a tantrum
So much better, to be in the anthem
Love who you are, increase your immunity
Improve your health and enhance your community

Too much emotion, disturbs an ocean
Better get the notion, of love and devotion
Just say this, you can do no wrong
with an attitude of gratitude, love going along

CHORUS...

I've got an attitude
Of love and gratitude
It's not just a platitude
It's the real thing

...

...
You know that coke, gives you a stroke
Hostile thinking does the same thing
I don't need this, to get my bliss
Just an attitude of gratitude and a loving kiss

It's nothing addictive or restrictive
Forget past history, get in the mystery
No interruption, done without corruption
Just L&G, the way to live

Being in the attitude of love and gratitude
Makes you a winner, well before dinner
Forget being rude, be a cool dude
There is no disaster, you will be master,

Try it, buy it, it's better than diet
You can be king, with just one thing,
An attitude of gratitude and your heart will sing

CHORUS...

I've got an attitude
Of love and gratitude
It's not just a platitude
It's the real thing

NINA TABARES

*G*rew up in the Andes Mountains of South America. The beauty of the Andes filled her with love and appreciation for nature while providing the perfect canvas to develop her talent.

At age sixteen, she began painting spending a year as a new bride exploring the Amazon River and surrounding lakes and tributaries on a house- boat. During this once in a lifetime experience, she was inspired by the beauty of the Rainforest, which influence her later wildlife art.

She had the unique opportunity to draw and paint all over the country while touring with her husband who was in the U.S. Navy. She is an accomplished artist winning numerous awards. Her paintings have been displayed in museums, galleries and exhibitions in different parts of the country.

She came to visit Washington State and after viewing the Cascade Mountains which reminded her of the native Andes of her childhood she decided to make Washington her home.

mayani@tabares.org

ONE DAY OF FISHING

The morning seemed to be promising. I had been invited to go fishing at dawn and the anxiety was filling my soul. I woke up a few times during the night to look at the clock until the alarm finally rang at 3:30 a.m.

It was time to get up. I showered quickly and got dressed in my jeans, a sweater, a jacket, and my tennis shoes. I grabbed my gloves and went downstairs to the kitchen just in time -- my friend was arriving at the door. He came in and, after I made fresh coffee, I got the fishing box where I had previously packed some food and we left towards the lake.

The golden lights of the truck were breaking the shadows of the road. Above us and at a distance, the firmament was saturated with thousands of stars. We did not talk; we listened to the radio and sipped our warm coffee. In my mind I was greeting the new day and waiting in anticipation to discover its wonders.

Finally, after passing some small hills and a group of houses, we turned down a road that was surrounded by luxurious fir trees. This road would take us to our destination. We left the truck near some rocks. Daniel, my friend, put his red canoe over his shoulders. I got the fishing poles and bait the boxes, and we both walked down the narrow, crooked and slippery path between the blackberry bushes towards the landing edge of the lake.

I had been there before and knew the way, but still I was walking carefully: by then the shadows were breaking with the light of dawn.

"Look!" he told me when he was putting the canoe over the water; a shadow passed over us at the same time that we heard an immense murmur of wings.

"Oh!" I said, smiling.

Each one of us sat in our places in the canoe and we began to row toward the east. I was at the front because I was not too experienced. We had been rowing for about five minutes going away from the edge of the lake when thousands of small birds came flying low over the water and over us. I was looking at them, fascinated.

"They are having their breakfast of mosquitoes," Daniel said. "The others were bats."

"Oh, both were pretty amazing."

The light of dawn was growing, lightly dissipating the shadows by the time we were in the middle of the lake. I was looking with attention at the water, taking care to row without touching the tips of the trees, which were lying submerged, motionless, and erect, seemingly sleeping an eternal dream.

We were rowing towards our left across the lake towards the mouth of the river from which it fed. From time to time, I would raise my eyes to look at the horizon, looking for our place of destination. Then I saw with anxiety the dense fog that was coming toward us.

I look at Daniel who was rowing behind me and I noticed he was not showing any concern. I did not say anything and looked ahead again.

The fog was coming, white and dense, and like a blanket, was covering the crystal clear waters, the plants, and everything around. I breathed deeply the pure air and got ready to receive it. The morning felt fresh. Passing by, the fog felt surprisingly warm; it covered me with an ethereal and ineffable touch, and I felt caressed and kissed on my forehead, my lips, and cheeks. A sweeter caress I have never felt before.

We kept advancing, leaving behind the fog, which was moving swiftly on its own. Ahead of us, not far, was our place of destination: the yellow lily pads.

Small groups of plants were floating near the edge of the lake; the water was still. We decided to stop rowing in a clear area and got the fishing poles ready. Daniel, who was proud of his abilities as a fisherman, wanted to show me some of his techniques and almost always caught a fish, but after taking the lures out of them, he would put them back into the water.

I was just happy to cast the line well, although by now I had learned enough from him and caught a few fish.

When fishing, people do not like to talk. I began thinking to myself: Why do fish let themselves get caught more than one time? You can tell some have been caught before. Why does Daniel have such passion for fishing but more for catching bass? Is it because the bass are warriors? What in the world, are those huge balloon-like things floating underwater under the trees? I cannot believe that bird attacked the eagle when she caught a fish.

Be careful, little bird. I remembered a dream I had some time ago about an eagle flying from behind a big bull, grabbing him from the neck up the air like a feather, and placing him sprawled over a branch of a tree.

I still remember the astonished look of the bull, and the strength and power of the eagle. I like to fish, but that of taking the lures out of fishes' mouths is not exciting; fish is too slippery and I have a hard time doing that.

When our knees and legs became stiff after having been sitting down for about two hours, we went up to shore. The edge of the lake was full of weeds and brush, but we found an area nearby with maples and fir trees. There, a thick carpet of moss that looked like green velvet covered the ground. I took my shoes off and walked on it feeling its freshness and smoothness. The roots of some of the trees around were overgrown, exposed, and entangled. We sat on one that looked comfortable and had some coffee, fruit, and a sandwich. Talked and smiled enjoying that fine morning and after a while we went back to our canoe.

The morning was now clear of fog, and the sun was shining over the water. We rowed again and got close to an area full of lily pads. Fish love to swim around them. The plants were lotuses, but wild lotuses, not the gentle ones that grow in so many city lakes in the surrounding parks. These lotuses were luxurious, their leaves were crooked, twisted, showing an indomitable spirit; their fragrance was strong and their flowers were more like an inverted bell. Flowers were all over, poking out from within the twisted leaves. Steam was flowing out of the water between and around the lily pads as well as the aroma of wildflowers. A feeling of energy and strength was all around.

Above the flowers, flew dragonflies. I saw that day some of the most beautiful cerulean blue and red dragonflies. I have always loved them, but seeing them there in the wild touching the water at times and doing some strange curbs flying was fascinating.

I bent down to get a flower; Daniel also cut some for me. I admired their beautiful medium yellow petals with bright red bottom backs.

Coming back, Daniel said,

   " Here,"

And he gave me a dead yellow dragonfly.

   " I found it on a leaf."

The yellow dragonfly wings were shimmering gold in the sunlight.

We got back without any fish, but my hands were full of color and my soul of wonderment.

RAINFOREST

$\mathcal{I}$'m a continuous circle or rebirth
Given from my womb life to fauna and flora.
My breath of life is warm, wet, rich,
it shines in the dew of early morning,
and flows in the vapor of the swamps.
I move with the cadence of a panther
and of an ant.
My voice is the murmur of the leaves
the song of birds, crickets, and frogs.
I am the caretaker of the land
Rain Forest I'm called

TO A GROWN CHILD

It only takes an instant to remember
the time when you arrived,
I can see you helpless, and fragile
smiling in my arms.

My eager thoughts about your future
seamed far away, but very important then,
and as an uncertain adventure
life moved and went ahead.

The times that seemed far then
have silently arrived.
You have grown, and on your own
You hold your future in your hands.

I can see in the images of my mind
all the faces and facets as you grew.
Those days have been too short, perhaps
and there are no regrets.

You have sprinkled my life
all of these years with sweet spices,
and the delightful aroma of your being
will always be along
into the sacred treasures of my soul.

WITHIN

Being quiet in my meditation
I heard a loud noise
along with that, I heard a sound of music
and a sound of bells
a sound of water rushing
a sound of a waterfall
it was a welcoming sound.
The loud sound of my heart beating
and millions of tiny bells
thanking my presence deep within.
My blood rushing like a river
a happy sound of life
seamed to flow like a sweet melody
into the walkways
and corridors of myself.

FREEDOM

is

a state of mind

it's the result of breaking away

self-imposed chains

to our reasoning.

www.ingramcontent.com/pod-product-compliance
Lightning Source LLC
Chambersburg PA
CBHW060927180626
46817CB00004B/1432